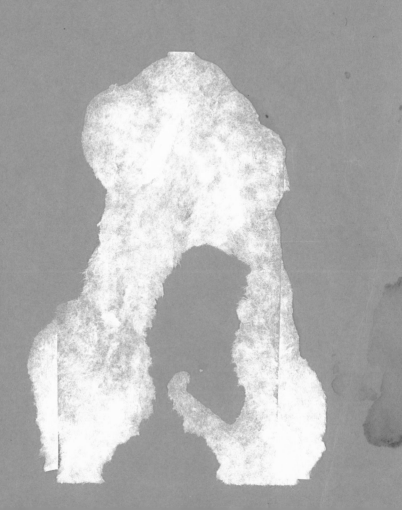

Women Are from Pluto,
Men Are from Uranus

A PARODY

Women Are from Pluto

MEN ARE FROM URANUS

(not to be confused with Men Are from Mars, Women Are from Venus)

The Big Bang and Other Premature Theories of Love

MIKE NICHOLS

THE SUMMIT PUBLISHING GROUP • ARLINGTON, TEXAS

THE SUMMIT PUBLISHING GROUP
One Arlington Centre
1112 East Copeland Road
Fifth Floor
Arlington, Texas 76011

Printed in the United States of America.

00 99 98 97 96   010   5 4 3 2 1

Library of Congress Cataloging-in-Publication Data

Nichols, Mike,1949-
    Women are from Pluto, men are from Uranus : the big bang and
other premature theories of love / by Mike Nichols.
        p. cm.
    ISBN 1-56530-224-9
    1. Man-woman relationships. 2. Love. 3. Sex differences
(Psychology) 1. Title.
HQ801.N515 1996
306.7--dc20   96-35685
                                                         CIP

Cover and book design by David Sims
Illustrations by Dan Clayton

To the lowly earthworm, who,
having both male and female genders in one body,
can take itself to the senior prom

Contents

Prologue:
It's D'lightful, It's D'lovely, It's D'capitated viii

1   ORIGINS:
Mister and Myth 2

2   LOVE:
Cupid's Beaus and Eros 14

3   SEX:
Once upon a Hormone 28

4   WOMEN:
I Am Woman, Hear Me Taupe 42

5   MEN:
He-Man, Hee-Haw 58

6   DATING:
The Single File 74

7   AGING:
Life's Three—Or, We Hope, Four—Seasons 90

8   COMMUNICATION:
Well, Shut My Mouth! 112

9   TROUBLE:
Love's Labor's Lester 128

Epilogue:
United We Stand, Divided We Pay Divorce Lawyers . . . 154

It's D'lightful, It's D'lovely, It's D'capitated

IN THE following pages we will turn our undivided attention to women (and the men who love them), men (and the women who love them), the darned fool ways they both act at times, what makes them happy (i.e., their attraction to each other), and what makes them unhappy (i.e., their attraction to each other).

Women and men are—as you know if you paid any attention at all during puberty—very, very different. To illustrate just how different women and men are, consider your response to this touching scene of entomological romance:

> *In the insect world, as a male and a female praying mantis are mating, the female bites off the head of the male. Despite his mortal injury, the male continues to perform, completing the act of sex before dying.*

How you respond to that scene probably will be determined by your gender:

If you are a man, you may snort and say: "Hah! That sounds just like a woman!"

If you are a woman, you may snort and say: "Hah! That sounds just like a man!"

And yet despite their differences, men and women, like praying mantises, do share the same goals. The first goal is love—that magical, indefinable bond that inspires in a man and a woman romance, devotion, and tenderness.

The second goal is sex—that equally magical, indefinable bond that inspires in a man and a woman the urge to rip each other's clothes off at a formal reception.

Under ideal circumstances, first comes love, then sex, then the attempt to fish your cummerbund out of the crystal punch bowl.

Ah, but men and women define their goals differently and go about reaching them differently. Take their primary goal— that of love. Men and women want different things out of it, put different things into it, react differently to the highs and lows of it. Those differences can cause us pain, frustration, and confusion. They can cause us to eat too much and drink too much. The next thing we know, we're trying to hijack a Häagen-Dazs truck armed only with a bottle of Thunderbird.

But just imagine a world without differences, without variety and contrasting opinions.

Imagine a world where the only color is gray.

Or where the only musical note is B-flat.

Or where everyone is five foot one. Why, just the bloody sales riots in petite departments would be horrific.

Men and women: two very different genders seeking the very same things. Wow, does that promise some fun or what!?

Or, as the male praying mantis expressed it so eloquently: "Arrrrrgghh-h-h-h-h-h…"

OTHER BOOKS BY MIKE NICHOLS

Life and Other Ways to Kill Time

Real Men Belch Downwind:
Modern Etiquette for the Primitive Man

CHAPTER One

Origins: Mister and Myth

TO COMPREHEND the profound differences between men and women, imagine that the two genders originally lived on separate planets and that each gender had no idea that the other gender even existed. Women lived on Pluto; men lived on Uranus.

Uranus! It was a huge planet, a remote planet, a planet whose name triggered involuntary snickering throughout the solar system.

Uranus also was a rough and rugged planet, peopled with rough and rugged men. Men were an aggressive gender. Men had fights; men fought wars. Men resolved conflicts with fists, handguns, knives, tanks, bombs. They had conventional bombs and atomic bombs. They also had neutron bombs that would kill the enemy but leave the enemy's golf courses intact.

Because there were no women on Uranus, no children were born. Instead, babies—all of them male— just seemed to appear. The men of Uranus had no idea where these babies came from. Nor did the men show much imagination in naming these babies—every person on Uranus was named Mel. But the name seemed to fit. Deep inside, each man and boy somehow felt like a Mel.

HOME SWEET HOME

The baby Mels were raised, in a clumsy way, by their elders. The babies were fed a formula of Gatorade and pureed Slim Jims and diapered in old chamois cloths. The bull pens of baseball stadiums served as communal nurseries until the boys were old enough to take care of themselves—usually age four or the seventh inning, whichever came first.

Because the men of Uranus had no women or romance or sex in their world, when they were not fighting, they poured their energy into building and creating and achieving. They created great and lasting works of art and literature. Poets wrote deeply personal sonnets, but they were sonnets about roping calves or gigging frogs or overhauling engines ("Hey, Mel, what rhymes with 'carburetor'?").

Men built mighty bridges and towering skyscrapers. They built projects in their home workshops. They climbed the tallest mountains and crossed uncharted oceans. They bowled.

Other sports were just as popular, especially contact sports. Earning a letter for athletics in high school entitled a man to burial with honors in the national cemetery, alongside veterans of the military and VCR repairmen.

When men played sports, they were very competitive. They loved to win. They hated to lose. But play-ing, and even winning, was not as much fun with-out someone special to show off for, to excel in front of, to impress, to validate their prowess.

When they excelled, it was exciting but not fully satisfying, like when you see extraterrestrials land in your backyard, but there are no other witnesses.

Without women around, men did not pay much attention to their appearance. They didn't shave on a daily basis, didn't keep their shoes shined, and trimmed their toenails only on religious holidays.

The men of Uranus were an uninhibit-ed bunch. Flatulence was considered a tal-ent, and sometimes a part for it was written into classical scores by Beethoven and Tchaikovsky.

On TV, reruns of *Starsky and Hutch* were on twenty-four hours a day; Jean-Claude Van Damme had his own talk show. In the federal government, a master brewer and a master mechanic held cabinet positions (secretary of hops and secretary of vroom vroom, respectively).

The men of Uranus thought that they had full, happy lives—lives filled with good-natured punching of shoulders, changing of spark plugs, and mounting of stuffed fish on walls.

But sometimes the men did sense a void—such as when they had a party. The men always showed up, carrying corsages that they never gave to anyone. Then they just slouched along the walls of the gym with their hands in their pockets until the party was over. They never danced together, even though they had hired a dance band (Mel and his Four Mels).

Then one day, in an eerie portent of things to come, Mel—a bespectacled, geeky guy whom the other Mels considered to be an eccentric—invented a skimpy two-piece bit of cloth and elastic that he called a "bikini." The other men of Uranus thought he was weird. "What's that for?" and "What do you do with it?" they asked him with scorn, although the sight of this "bikini" thing did arouse men in a way that they could not explain. With a visionary gleam in all four eyes, Mel the inventor stared off into the vastness of space and said, "I just have a hunch that someday… "

SUGAR AND SPICE AND CELLULITE

Meanwhile, millions of miles away, unbeknownst to the men of Uranus, were the women of Pluto. Pluto was a dainty planet, and the women had worked hard to make it the most tastefully decorated planet in the solar system. There were mountain ranges made of mauve throw pillows and valleys upholstered with delicate pastel prints. There was no dust on the entire planet. Even the deserts were vacuumed twice a week.

Compared with Uranus, Pluto was a peaceful place. Women responded to words of anger with words of anger, not with violence. There were no wars or fistfights, although when two women or two groups of women were terribly upset with each other, one might, in uncontrollable rage, belittle the other's ability to accessorize.

Women, in their world without men, stayed very busy and had full, productive lives. Women were not repressed or stereotyped. There were no gender roles. Women were free to be whatever they wanted to be. They had careers in every field. They were butchers, bakers, and candlestick makers, welders and bull riders and plumbers and doctors and politicians and accountants and even secretaries.

Away from their work, women had seemingly full social lives. They did lunch—white wine and salads in trendy cafés with art prints on the walls. They swapped recipes. They shopped. They gardened, read, wrote letters, owned boutiques. Women appreciated opera and ballet and the symphony. They had a thriving public television network. They had book review clubs and junior leagues; they did volunteer work for many worthwhile causes. On national holidays they had telethons for split ends, cellulite, and yeast infections.

Because there were no men, women could not have children, so they adopted. And lo, there were no stretch marks. This caused much rejoicing. All the children were girls, and the women showed much imagination and variation in naming them: Shandra, Tara, Ashley, Cindy, Cyndi, Cyndee. The women were very fulfilled by nurturing these baby girls. In school, the girls did well in math and science because no one told them they could not. They took wood shop and metal shop but at graduation ceremonies were still able to receive their diplomas with all five fingers.

Women felt free to spit and curse and belch and scratch themselves, but they seldom saw any need to.

The women of Pluto played sports, too. But women, although competitive, did not overemphasize winning. They liked to win, but because of their sense of empathy took little satisfaction in defeating an opponent. They were as proud of a 71–71 tie as of a 71–0 rout.

On Pluto, women cooperated as much as they competed. Women did not keep their feelings to themselves, and they seldom felt their sexuality threatened. Unlike the men of Uranus, the women of Pluto danced together when they had parties and no one thought it weird or funny.

Women paid a lot of attention to their appearance because it was important to their self-esteem. Oh, you might see a woman with some minor grooming flaw, such as having her blouse not neatly tucked in or having a chipped fingernail. But such oversights were rare and usually made the evening news ("Woman seen with run in pantyhose. Film at eleven").

The women of Pluto were as happy as they could be, they thought.

But then one day a strong solar wind blew straight out of downtown Destiny. The astronomers of Pluto and Uranus, working independently, invented powerful telescopes. Soon they discovered each other's planets and began to observe the inhabitants. As men watched the women they immediately felt strange, new stirrings. Their hearts pounded. Their nostrils flared. Suddenly they no longer looked at their power tools with the same fondness. Likewise, women on Pluto were equally attracted to the men they saw on Uranus. They felt warm flushes. Suddenly they began to wonder what it might be like to dance with someone who didn't smell of Maybelline and Massengill.

On both planets, the populations shouted: "*Yes!* We *knew* there was something missing!" and executed simultaneous worldwide "high fives" that measured 5.6 on the Richter scale.

In no time, the two planets began to communicate via powerful radios. Soon they had even more ambitious plans: a rendezvous in space—a massive interplanetary blind date.

The women of Pluto sent a message to the men of Uranus: "Bring examples of your finest music, art, literature, and philosophy."

The men of Uranus sent a message to the women of Pluto: "Bring beer."

And so the astroengineers of Pluto and Uranus built spaceships capable of reaching a rendezvous point between the two planets. The women's spaceship was utilitarian, designed to do the job, yet tasteful. It had a 12,000-horsepower nuclear engine and chintz curtains. The men's spaceship was overpowered, thick and long, with loud mufflers and orange flames painted on the sides.

At last came the great day of the rendezvous. Amid much anticipation, on each planet the launch coordinator performed the countdown: "Five, four, three, two, one, beach blanket bingo!"

LOVE: THE FINAL FRONTIER

But in space, as the two ships approached each other and were about to dock, something went horribly wrong. Witnesses disagreed about what happened. The women said the men neglected to signal a turn. The men said the women had no brake lights. Thus did history record the first time that men and women disagreed. Anyway, the two ships collided in the inky infinity of space. Many were confused, disoriented, and hurt, thus setting the tone for male-female relations for all time.

The two wrecked ships, their bumpers locked, drifted far away from their home planets for years, finally crash-landing on the planet Earth. Both genders found the Earth's atmosphere tolerable and proclaimed it a neutral place for their shared regenesis.

The landing on Earth was fortuitous for all concerned. Pluto, the women's planet, was quickly filling up with discarded go-go boots from the '60s, and Uranus, the men's planet, was developing an unhealthful level of methane from centuries of uninhibited flatulence. It had reached the point that men were afraid to light a match. Instead, they made fire by rubbing two Boy Scouts together.

At a formal ceremony dedicating the new home and the new relationship between men and women, the elected representative of the men, Mel, said, with gravity and grace, "We, the men of Uranus, welcome the women of Pluto to our common new home and extend our pledge of friendship, support, cooperation, and stewardship for the fulfillment of all."

The elected representative of the women responded with: "Does this dress make me look fat?"

When at long last the men of Uranus and the women of Pluto got together, it was a bittersweet turning point for both. They had crossed the Rubicon of romance. Life would never be the same again. It was like the fall from grace in Genesis, when Adam and Eve ate the fruit of the tree of knowledge of good and evil, and suddenly they looked down and saw that they were not only naked but also anatomically correct.

Ignorance had been bliss. Now the men formerly of Uranus cared if they lost their hair. Now the women formerly of Pluto cared even more if their hair was mussed. They realized that they had been living a shadow life, going through the motions, stumbling zombielike.

But it also was a delightful period of adjustment and learning. Each gender taught the other. Men taught women how to deaden the bat when laying down a bunt. Women taught men that Tchaikovsky's *1812 Overture* could sound even better with cannon.

Then, one night, a man and a woman discovered sex under circumstances that are unknown (although historians theorize that it involved a six-pack and a Kenny G. album).

As news of sex spread, instantly men forgot about their workshops and sports and battlefields. Women, too, ignored their former pursuits. The economy faltered, factories were idled. For the first few weeks after the discovery of sex, the streets of Earth were deserted. People got naked and stayed that way. People didn't even come out of their bedrooms, except maybe to go to the front door to embarrass the bejeebers out of a Jehovah's Witness. Come Monday and time to go back to work, millions of male and female employees stayed home and called in horny.

Months later, babies began to be born. And none of them was named Mel.

But you can't stay in bed and make love the rest of your life, although God knows we've all tried.

After couples emerged from their musky homes, at theaters everyone wanted to sit in the balcony; at restaurants everyone wanted the intimate, dimly lit corner tables. Waiters began auctioning off these tables, which went for as much as one thousand dollars, but for that you also got bread sticks and refills on coffee.

Under the euphoric spell of love and sex, people who were forty felt twenty again, people who were sixty felt forty again, people who were eighty felt sixty again but found sixty to be no huge improvement and went back to feeling eighty.

Lovers strolled hand in hand and barefoot through spring showers. They skipped. They frolicked. But the muscles that are used to frolic—located near the muscles that are used to cavort—were weak from years of disuse, and lovers were awkward and uncoordinated, like Republicans trying to perform "the wave."

And dancing was a travesty. The couples had no rhythm. On a dance floor, a simple waltz could send dozens to the emergency room.

There were other adjustments. The two genders had never had lovers with whom to trade terms of endearment and baby talk. Thus "Mel's Little Angel Eyes" or "Cyndee's Honey Buns" had to evolve from clumsy attempts such as "Mel's Little Toggle Bolt" and "Cyndee's Great Big Fondue Fork."

Back on their separate, monogender planets men and women had formed relationships, of course—many close and lasting relationships. But they were platonic. Between friends. Between coworkers. But men and women quickly found that love is to friendship what a lightning bolt is to a joy buzzer. Love, they found, is friendship dipped in chocolate and sprinkled with stardust and gunpowder.

But men and women also found that it was a lot harder to get along with a lover than with a bridge partner or a fishing buddy. If you have a spat with a fishing buddy, you can just cast from the other side of the boat. If you have a spat with a lover and cast from the other side of the bed, all you'll catch is grief and dust bunnies.

After the honeymoon period, men and women realized that the two genders were different beyond the obvious—and celebrated—physical differences. Men and women, they found, think differently, feel differently, communicate differently.

Those differences are manageable in a friendship. But romance is a horse of a different lipstick color.

Certainly men and women approached love from different places. Men were logical, but love defies logic, and that frightened men. Unlike a fishing reel or an alternator or a computer, love was something men could not control. They could not take love apart, analyze it, solve it, and figure out how it works (and even if they could, after they put it back together they probably would have some parts left over).

But women, because they were more intuitive and grounded in emotion, embraced the mystery, the chemistry of love.

Women embraced love *because* they couldn't explain it. Men embraced love *although* they couldn't explain it.

Men and women who were accustomed to merely platonic relationships were scarcely prepared for the dizzying highs and abysmal lows that romance brought. It made them giddy and pouty, as vulnerable as children.

With love, both genders had so much to gain, which meant they also had so much to lose.

Life was about to become very interesting for the women from Pluto and a bunch of guys named Mel.

Love: Cupid's Beaus and Eros

Love is heaven, and heaven is love
SIR WALTER SCOTT

*Love is only the dirty trick played on us
to achieve continuation of the species*
SOMERSET MAUGHAM

WHAT DO the two quotations above tell us? First, they tell us that of the two men, Scott probably mailed out a lot more valentines each year. And second, they tell us that people regard love in powerful and sometimes contrasting ways.

And why not? Love is the most powerful force on earth. It is the nuclear fission of emotions. Who has not been transported to the heights of joy and the depths of depression by the vagaries of love? Who does not thrill at each heart thump, throat lump, and goose bump of love? Who has not marveled at its many forms? There is platonic love, same-sex love, love of country, love of money, love of chocolate. There is the love between parent and child, between brother and sister, between comrades-in-arms, between pet owner and pet. There is the love between a narcissist and his shaving mirror.

But it is romantic love between a man and a woman that we are concerned with in this book, because to most people

that is the most traditional, the most elusive, the most cherished, and the most likely to result in a man and a woman either sharing lifelong happiness or exchanging gunfire over the breakfast table.

At any given time, most of us are seeking love, reveling in love, or getting over love. Men and women have lied for it, died for it, built marble monuments to it, written sonnets about it, showered twice a day for it, crammed size-ten thighs into size-seven pants for it.

Love truly makes the world go around. Everyone wants to be loved. Skeptical? Ask any ten people on the street: "Do you want to be loved?" You will get nine replies of "yes" and one reply of "Right *now*? Right here on the street? How about during lunch, back at my place? You bring the cream cheese."

HERE'S LOOKING AT YOU, VERMIN

Love is a basic need. Experiments show that lab rats in a cage stocked with food and cocaine will eat the cocaine and ignore the food and eventually die. But if two lab rats that are in love with each other are put into a cage that is stocked with food and cocaine, they will ignore both the food *and* the cocaine until eventually they die, found one morning at 3 A.M. watching *Casablanca* on TV with their heads together and their tails entwined.

Love, and its randy little handmaiden, sex, permeate our thoughts and actions so thoroughly that we are not even aware of their influence most of the time. They influence how we dress, how we smell, what we drive, what we listen to, how we spend much of our time and money, our self-esteem. Love inspires timeless works of art and music. Love inspires men to learn to like dancing and inspires women to learn to pretend that they like fishing.

Our heartstrings make puppets of us all.

Love has brought down royal families, toppled governments, triggered wars. No wonder Cupid never goes anywhere anymore without a lawyer.

It's no wonder that we have looked for love everywhere—in drive-in theaters, on college campuses, office buildings, singles ads, malls, bars, church socials, in grade schools and nursing homes, at parties and at funerals. Sometimes we look in all the wrong places. Love is like a lost sock—it usually shows up in the last place you'd expect to find it.

Sometimes love is circumstantial. A seating chart at a sit-down dinner places you next to a total stranger. You and the stranger reach for the salt shaker at the same time, and the tips of your fingers touch lightly, just like in that creation scene on the ceiling of the Sistine Chapel. You both think, "If this isn't a sign, I don't know what is." You catch your breath. Your eyes meet. A chill runs down your entree.

Sometimes love is ironic. Two coworkers may not particularly like each other and may, in fact, have the sort of relationship in which they routinely exchange letter bombs through interoffice mail. But to their surprise, one day they find that opposites do indeed attract and that with time and tolerance and lack of pressure to *make* love happen, they have developed a mutual respect and an appreciation that lead to lingering, passionate trysts at the office photocopy machine:

She: "Oh, Tyrone, I love the way you caress the 'paper size' selector button."

He: "Oh, Ramona, was it 8 1/2 by 11 for you, too?"

Clearly, a world without love would be barren, sterile, merely platonic. Without love, women would meet just for lunch. Without love, men would meet just for league softball. In spring a young man's fancy would lightly turn to thoughts of groin pulls. Without love, men would stop shaving their faces, women would stop shaving their legs. The world would be a far fuzzier place.

LOVE AND THE GNP

Without love, imagine the loss just to the economy. Yes, predictably, love has spilled out of our bedrooms, backseats, lovers' lanes, and theater balconies to become big business. Each year billions are spent on the traps and trappings of love: breath mints, makeup, mood music, alluring clothing, fragrances, flowers, greeting cards, candy, satin sheets, contraceptives, diamond rings, weddings, wedding gifts, counselors, divorce lawyers. Without love, singles bars would become vast wastelands, dust on their tables, cobwebs on their beer taps, tumbleweeds blowing across their floors where once sincere single people hoped to find that certain someone to love until the end of time or at least until breakfast.

Without love, Paris would be just another city with rude people and creamy sauces.

Without love, crooners such as Barry White and Bing Crosby would have been on welfare.

Barry: "Hey, Bing, I got some government cheese. Want some?"

Bing: "Oh, Ba-Ba-Ba-Barry!"

Without love, on Valentine's Day, out-of-work Hallmark writers would wander the land, holding up signs that read:

"No one buys cards.
No one gets wooed.
Please help me, Pard:
Will rhyme for food."

Okay, so love is powerful and has something to do vaguely with cheese and someone named Pard. But what, exactly, *is* love? The skeptical, analytical scientist would say, as did Maugham, that love is no more than a biochemical mechanism that serves to perpetuate the species (gee, and scientists wonder why they aren't invited to more parties).

After all, the scientist would reason, if people don't fall in "love," they don't procreate. If they don't procreate, the human race ceases to exist. And with no more people, the planet Earth would be a very different place. The so-called lower animals soon would take over our deserted cities. And you just *know* that they'd let our malls become understocked.

Surely love must be more than Maugham's cynical assessment of it; and yet the brightest minds through the ages have failed to define it. Plato, Shakespeare, and Freud struggled in vain. So did St. Thomas Aquinas and Immanuel Kant. As did Confucius, who admitted that he didn't know what love is but that "whatever it is, it should come with a fortune cookie."

Love is perhaps best understood not in terms of what it *is*, but rather in terms of what it *does*.

And love does the wackiest things.

Love makes two strangers lock eyes across a crowded bar. Suddenly the room begins to spin. It becomes a centrifuge with drapes. She hears angels sing. He hears music. Possibly because he has just put a quarter into the jukebox.

Love makes us act against our better judgment. After dating someone for just a week, we suddenly realize: "This is happening too fast. We gotta slow down." But then we tumble headlong anyway. By the second week we have made a down payment on adjoining cemetery plots.

Love makes us giddy with our good fortune. When two people are knee-deep in gaga, they succumb to the urge to rush outside at 2 A.M. and run down the block knocking on doors and yelling: "He loves me." "And she loves me." "I love her." "And I love him." "We love each other." "I'm his." "And she's mine."

Soon the two of them collapse on the sidewalk in a mass of pulsating pronouns.

Love makes every single thing you see or hear remind you of your lover. That thing might have nothing to do with him or her, but your brain will find an association. For example, you are in love with a big lug named Charles. You are driving along and come to a stop sign. "Stop" makes you think of its opposite: "Go." That's spelled "G-O." "G" and "O" are Georgia O'Keeffe's initials. This makes you think of cow skulls. Which reminds you of hamburger. Which reminds you of ground chuck. Ground chuck! Of course—once when Charles was in the air force and used his F-16 to go for pizza, the Pentagon's order to his commanding officer was "Ground Chuck!"

LOVE AMONG THE GOOBERS

Love makes the tiniest coincidences assume deep significance. Two people who are still learning about each other delight in each thing that they have in common: "You like peanut butter? Man, this is too weird! *I* like peanut butter!" This discovery is followed by much smiling and sighing. The two of them begin to make plans for a lifetime together, beginning with a honeymoon at the Peter Pan factory.

When you are in love, you feel that your entire life to this point has been prologue, mere preparation for this preordained moment. Your pleasure is almost painful. You are convinced that never before in the history of the human race have two people been so much in love, felt these feelings so deeply. But in actuality, of course, couples in love have had those very same feelings since the beginning of time. Our earliest ancestors—just one-celled organisms—had the very same feelings as they slithered up out of the primordial ooze of the sea and one cooed to the other:

"Your tide pool or mine?"

Love can turn the most nimble mind to mush. When Shakespeare met Anne Hathaway, he was so smitten, so distracted, that his literary IQ plummeted. In his first version of *Hamlet*, Polonius was a maple tree. Shakespeare finally regained his senses and rewrote the part of Polonius, but by then audiences at the Globe Theater had become accustomed to seeing Polonius's leaves turn.

Love causes people to become disoriented, unable to concentrate. For this reason, people in love should not be allowed to drive. People in love just sorta tend to drive straight ahead for great distances until they run out of gas or hit a curb, usually somewhere in Iowa. The governor of Iowa has recently declared the entire state a tow-away zone.

The irony is that even though love is such an important human need, we enter into it so rashly. Sometimes it doesn't take much to trigger love: a man's superficial charm, a woman's Tiffany tinkle of laughter, a beefy bicep, a bosom that could provide shade to an entire Scout troop.

He Said, She Said

Pierre Curie: "Sure, Marie discovered radium. You know how? I know how. I was there helping her. She was making bouillabaisse one night and added too much pepper. The bouillabaisse began to glow. That's when she discovered radium. That's also when I suggested that we eat out."

(Behind every successful woman is a man handing her fish.)

Phil Donahue fell for Marlo Thomas while watching reruns of *That Girl*. It was her legs that first made his pulse race. Little did Phil know that the TV studio used a double for those close-ups of Marlo's legs. The legs that Phil saw and fell for actually belonged to Rhonda Jean Blevins, an otherwise unattractive and surly woman who has since left Hollywood to run a combination wig and muffler shop in Nebraska.

We may spend weeks researching the purchase of a home or a tennis racket, but we may fall—nay, *leap*—in love in a matter of minutes. For example, you get into an elevator on the first floor of a department store.

"Four, please," you say to a total stranger who is already in the elevator. As the door slides closed, something about that stranger interests you.

By the third floor, you are downright fascinated.

And one floor later: "Ding!" Was that the elevator bell or your heart?

Everyone out. Fourth floor: sporting goods, linens, housewares.

Because you're in the neighborhood anyway, the two of you decide to pick out your silver pattern.

Mother Goose Update

> **As I was going to St. Ives**
> **I met a man with seven wives.**
> **Every wife had seven sacks,**
> **Every sack had seven cats,**
> **Every cat had seven kits.**
> **Kits, cats, sacks, and wives,**
> **How many were going to St. Ives?**

ST. IVES—A local man has been sentenced to prison after being found guilty of bigamy and leash law violations.

The suspect had turned himself in to police, begging officers to save him from his home life, which he described as "unbearable."

"It got to be intolerable," the man said. "Such hissing and yowling and scratching and fighting and licking their fur. And then there's the cats!

"I don't know how it got out of hand," he said about having so many wives and cats. "I guess I just didn't keep count. Forty-nine cats and seven wives! I was having to work two jobs and rob liquor stores at night just to get enough money for Kitty Litter and tampons."

When the judge sentenced the defendant to seven years in prison, the defendant began to weep and said he would appeal and ask a higher court for a life sentence.

Of course, anything that can lift us so high can also dash us to the ground ruthlessly. The first step taken along the path of love is often a false step. In the beginning, people both present and perceive each other inaccurately. People are so charming, so accommodating and lovable when they meet and fall in love—sometimes unnaturally so. People can't keep up that level of charm for long. They might injure themselves.

Sometimes this elevated level of charm is deliberate; sometimes it is unconscious. Regardless, it wears off. For example, at first it seems to a woman that her man likes to go out—dancing, dining, and clubbing. Six months later all he wants to do is stay home and watch TV—shows about people who go dancing, dining, and clubbing.

THE BIG CHILL

Or at first it seems to a man that his woman enjoys going with him to hockey games. Six months later, she claims to have developed a morbid fear of ice and, in fact, believes that she is being stalked by a giant Slurpee.

In both cases, these people have used up their allotment of charm. If they had continued to be charming at that level, they'd have had nothing left for their golden years.

Okay, so love is blind. But sometimes love pokes its own eyes out. Love doesn't *want* to see. For example, in your bliss, you ignore little flaws in your mate. And if you *do* see those little flaws, you rationalize them away. It will clear up, you tell yourself, like some kind of cold sore on that person's personality. "Okay, so he's a bit insecure. I find it kinda endearing. He'll grow out of it," you think. "So what if when we're out he won't let me go to the ladies' room unless I leave a security deposit with him. Who needs their Visa card in the john? I don't do that much shopping in there anyway."

Whereas a man thought a woman was "down to earth" when they met, he later realizes she is "dull." Whereas a woman thought that a man was "frugal" and "charmingly quiet" when they met, she later realizes he is, in fact, "cheap" and "comatose."

Or after the first blush of love, two people begin to suspect that they really don't have that much in common, and that two people cannot, in fact, build a deep and lasting relationship around having matching "Party 'til You Puke" T-shirts.

Sometimes your blindness causes you to fall in love with the wrong person. Everyone else sees it but you. Your parents tell you: "He's not right for you." Your friends tell you: "He's not right for you." A hoodlum comes up as the two of you are walking on a dark street, points a gun at you, takes your purse and watch, and tells you: "He's not right for you."

A month later, as you identify the hoodlum in a police lineup, you scream: "I hope you get fifty years, creep. And I shoulda listened to you."

Love has a rugged terrain. Peaks and valleys are its natural topography. All too often, while men and women are riding side by side through one of those valleys, they make a discovery. The man realizes that his woman is a puzzle in pantyhose. The woman realizes that her man is an enigma with ear hair.

Things begin to go wrong. And when they do, even sex, which is a powerful natural narcotic (heroin with hickeys), can do only so much to make things okay again.

Six weeks or six months or six years after they were so ecstatically in love, he and she find themselves arguing bitterly. Sometimes the issue is major: money, work, sex, the kids. Sometimes the issue is trivial, such as the setting on the electric blanket (he wants it set on "4," she wants it set on "cremate"). The situation deteriorates. The United Nations votes to step in. Peacekeeping troops are provided by the United States, Britain, and Germany, although France does send some croissants.

It is, sadly, a common pattern. The ability to maintain a healthy love relationship with another person is difficult.

And it is crucial to the mental health of both. It can even be a matter of life and death. These days unhealthy love results in messy divorces, stalking, domestic abuse, assault, even murder-suicides. Just read the newspapers: "Husband jailed in shooting of wife," "Ex-girlfriend held in vandalism of man's car," "Lovers' quarrel turns violent at steakhouse (Turn to 'Flying sirloin' on Page 2)."

The Doctor Is In

To help us better understand love, we close this chapter with the first of three house calls by Dr. Romance—the world-famous and highly respected (we're reading here from his tattoo) expert on love whose books on the subject are best-sellers (mainly because all of his ex-wives buy copies). Dr. Romance will answer questions that are commonly asked about love:

Q. Is there such a thing as love at first sight?

A. No, only infatuation at first sight. Real, true, lasting love develops with time, building up slowly but surely. Like floor wax.

Q. How many kinds of love are there?

A. There are thirty-seven known kinds of love, although scientists are working to develop a thirty-eighth— that between a fisherman and his night crawler.

Q. What is the difference between mature love and immature love?

A. Immature love is frantic, insecure, jealous, possessive. Let's say that a man is at the mall and catches a fleeting glimpse of his girlfriend and some man whom he does not recognize as the two disappear around a corner. An immature lover is stricken with jealousy and suspicion and either spies on the girl-friend or goes home to brood and fret.

In contrast, a mature lover goes about his business, perhaps casually asks his girlfriend the next time they talk who the man was—without a trace of negativity. That's mature love. No, wait, that's indifference. Dr. Romance always gets those two confused.

Q. **Why was Somerset Maugham so cynical about love?**

A. Because he had mailed a love letter to Gertrude Stein and she had just returned it to him with the grammar corrected.

CHAPTER Three

Sex: Once upon a Hormone

IF LOVE makes the world go around, surely sex oils the axis.

Sex is, without doubt, the single most crucial phenomenon in all of biology. After all, without sex:

Salmon would swim upstream and just loiter.

A queen bee would have to go out and get a *real* job.

On wedding nights, couples would get naked and just pick rice out of each other's hair.

Oh, and also, scientists say, life on Earth would cease to exist.

The allure of sex is surely the strongest in nature. Mother Nature really outdid herself with sex. If all she had wanted to do was ensure the perpetuation of the species, she could have given sex the attraction of a horseshoe magnet. Instead she gave sex the attraction of a black hole. Sex pulls everything into it—people, their time, their energy, their major credit cards. Sex—whether the general physical attraction between the two genders or the specific physical act between two people—plays an overwhelming role in our lives. It can redeem us. It can ruin us. It can make us crawl on our knees, howl at the moon, and write hot checks to Victoria's Secret.

We spend a good deal of our waking hours concerned with sex: how to achieve it, keep it in perspective, achieve it again as soon as possible, avoid it, pretend we did when we didn't,

pretend we did-
n't when we did,
pretend we want
to when we don't,
pretend we don't
want to when we
do, avoid it again,
achieve it again (this
time in an airplane),
dress for it, make it last longer,
get it over with sooner, keep our kids away from it,
and bribe the flight attendant not to report it.

Sex is a popular topic of conversation. For women, sex makes up a large part of what they talk about when they get together. And for men, sex is the lowest common denominator. No matter how old two or more males are, what their social or economic status is, what their backgrounds, politics, or value systems are, they will always be able to find common ground in their sexual attraction to women:

Chief justice of the U.S. Supreme Court: "Boy, that Kim Basinger. Homina homina homina!"

Fifteen-year-old pimply hoodlum: "You said it, Bill. Homina homina homina!"

Having bonded, later these two males go bowling together. The hoodlum rolls a 300, but this perfect score is overturned when Justice Rehnquist rules the fourth frame unconstitutional.

There is no end to the effort and imagination that people devote to sex—they ply each other with liquor, they "run out of gas" on deserted country roads. They play doctor, they play naked Scrabble and strip croquet. They have group sex, they check into cheap motels under an assumed libido. Teen boys come home from the prom at 5 A.M. smelling like a brothel and wearing just their underwear and explain to their parents: "There was an explosion at the Chanel factory, and I beat the flames out with my tuxedo."

It's truly fascinating what two people in the throes of sex *would* do, but it's also truly frightening what two people in the throes of sex would *not* do. They would not leave a burning building. They would not lend medical assistance to anyone who is not actually on the sofa with them at the time. They would not get up and answer the door no matter *how* many times Ed McMahon and Dick Clark knock.

Mother Goose Update

**Wee Willie Winkie runs through the town
Upstairs and downstairs, in his nightgown.**

YE OLDE LONDON TOWN—Wee W. Winkie was arrested for exhibitionism today after witnesses said that Mr. Winkie had been "flashing" for years, lifting his nightgown in public and claiming that "the wind blew it up."

He was ordered to undergo psychiatric evaluation, found to be "sane but naughty," and then charged with a felony by District Attorney Bo Peep. But after Winkie flashed D.A. Peep herself she took her eyewitness evidence into consideration and reduced the charge to a misdemeanor.

WHAT'S TOPS IN BOTTOMS

The standard of what is considered sexually attractive is fairly consistent throughout a given culture. In our culture, we value symmetrical facial features, prominent cheekbones, full lips, white teeth. The broad-at-the-shoulders, narrow-at-the-hips figure is the ideal for men. The hourglass figure is the ideal for women. Unlikely, but ideal.

Women appreciate several features in men: nice smile, strong chin, full head of hair. A set of washboard abs makes women want to scrub themselves clean. And they favor a small, compact bottom, a bottom that, if it were a singing group, would be Hall and Oates, not the Mormon Tabernacle Choir.

Men, on the other hand, are extremely interested in breasts. We men have founded major religions around breasts. It's one of those totally inexplicable but undeniable forces of nature. Like gravity. The intensity of this interest is hard to explain when you consider that breasts have never been more numerous. Let's

TOTALLY SHAVED PRIMATE DANCERS!

examine the numbers. There are about 250 million people in America. That means there are about 125 million women. That means there are about 250 million U.S. breasts. Now the United States has an area of 3,618,770 square miles. That's 69.08 breasts per square mile. A hundred years ago a man might live his entire life and never see a breast. He might have to be content with an artist's conception of a breast, drawn on a cocktail napkin and handed down to him by his father. But breasts are more visible than ever in today's relaxed moral climate. So you'd think that we guys would be accustomed to them by now and would be able, in a mature fashion, to get over them and turn our attention to matters that, in the cosmic scheme of an infinite universe, are perhaps a bit more significant.

Like legs.

He Said, She Said

Mrs. Pilgrim: "That Bo. In bed he always insists that I wear feathers and make clucking sounds. And I wish that just once that man would take off that damned silly hat of his."

In the name of sex, we men and women strive to make ourselves attractive to the opposite gender. We undergo silicone implants, collagen injections, hair plugs, face-lifts, tummy tucks, and nose jobs. We spend millions on cosmetics, hair colors, fragrances, lingerie, fast cars. We go to tanning salons, health spas, and gyms. We diet. We pump iron. We read *Cosmo*. We get bikini-waxed within an inch of our lives.

And then, when all our efforts are successful and someone indeed finds us sexually attractive, we whine, "Don't you like me for my mind?"

For a woman, interest in sex typically begins at age fourteen, remains strong past menopause, and slows down only when she discovers high-stakes bingo.

For a man, interest in sex typically begins at age thirteen and slows down only at rigor mortis.

After puberty kicks in, the sexual urge in humans is constant year-round, but it veritably throbs in the spring. This is only to be expected, considering that all winter long we have been bundled up in genderless, bulky coats, jackets, mufflers, snow boots, caps, gloves, and scarves. From November to March, it takes us so long to get undressed that we can mate only by appointment. But come spring and warmer weather, we wear less and start seeing some skin again. And it all comes back to us: boy, girl, touchy, feely. The sap rises. Hormones reach critical mass. On high school and college campuses, the sighting of the first pair of shorts overshadows the first robin. The mere sight of all those firm, rounded bodies can cause teenagers to enter puberty right in the middle of typing class, missing the teacher's stirring tribute to the shift key. Classes are skipped. Campus riots break out. Students abduct the dean of men and the dean of women, tie them together face-to-face, and force them to watch *9 1/2 Weeks*.

A SHORT—BUT VIRILE—HISTORY OF SEX

100,000 B.C.	Through a comical accident involving a man, a woman, and a nude sack race, early humans discover that sex is even better with *two* people.
80,000 B.C.	Bathing is invented.
50,000 B.C.	Kissing with *both* lips catches on.

April 40,001 B.C.	Sex found to cause pregnancy.
May 40,001 B.C.	Twin beds invented.
Dark Ages	Plague-carrying rats in bed are generally found to kill the mood.
A.D. 1245	Use of wooden condoms abandoned.
1892	Backseat invented.
1893	Car invented to make the backseat mobile.
1950s	Drive-in theaters flourish.
1960s	Deodorant takes the worry out of being close.
1980s	AIDS puts the worry back into being close.
1995	Two volunteers working backstage at a local PBS station hold a kiss during an entire pledge break. They eventually collapse from oxygen deprivation. Near death, they will their bodies to *Nova*.
1996	To help balance the budget, U.S. federal government opens a "976" phone sex line. When Sen. Jesse Helms proves to be the most popular operator, it is found that most calls are coming from tobacco lobbyists.

HISS AND HERS

Sex, of course, is closely related to love. The two—like the two snakes in the caduceus (the physician's insignia)—are tightly entwined. And if you think that the analogy between sex and love and two snakes is questionable, you've never seen two drunken anacondas on their honeymoon.

Sex is at its best, at its most fulfilling, when shared by two people who are in love. Of course, ideally, people in love don't "have sex." They make love. Big difference. Having sex is a purely physical act between two people who afterward may or may not compliment each other's nose rings. It is a churning, burning, reckless, writhing, nostril-flaring, toe-curling, teeth-grinding, eyelid-licking—there will now be a short pause while we hose down this paragraph.

On the other hand, making love is a deeply moving union that takes place between two people who love and respect each other very, very much and has about it a spiritual atmosphere that is not unlike being in church, the difference being that after making love, it is considered poor form to pass the collection plate.

Ideally, when people make love, lust and tenderness are in a beautiful dynamic tension. You are vulnerable one moment, invincible the next. You are equally eager to make squealing, wallpaper-peeling, head-over-heeling, rock-and-reeling love or to fall back and just cuddle. You don't really care which. It's a win-win situation—one of the few in life.

Just as there is a difference between having sex and making love, there is a difference between making love *with* and making love *to*. The prepositions are the key. *To* implies that one person is active and the other passive. One gives, the other receives. *With* implies balance, equity, participation. A person who is being made love *to* by someone can read a book at the same time. A person who is making love *with* someone would probably at least want to read out loud.

How to Tell "Making Love" from "Having Sex"

☛ It is making love if beforehand you insist on a lengthy and thorough period of acquaintance.

☛ It is having sex if beforehand you insist on an alias and a ski mask.

☛ It is making love if in the thick of it you whisper, "I think I am experiencing spiritual enlightenment."

☛ It is having sex if in the thick of it you whisper, "I think the trampoline is about to collapse."

☛ It is making love if afterward the two of you exchange tender, simultaneous sighs.

☛ It is having sex if afterward the two of you exchange business cards.

As you may have noticed, as with love, food, and everything else good that Mother Nature gives us, sex also has its bad side. Sex can be addictive. Sex can be used to control and manipulate. Sex can cause tension and hurt feelings and frustration among couples. One partner wants it less often, wants it more often, wants it with less talk, wants it with more talk, wants it with less tenderness, wants it with more tenderness, wants it with less humor, wants it with more humor but not necessarily a laugh track.

Sex can cause conflict when men and women regard it differently. For a woman, sex is apt to be a means to an end; for a man sex is more apt to be an end in itself. For a woman, sex is a physical union that allows two souls to merge into one. For a man, sex may well may be all that, but he is also pretty sure that two souls can merge into one better if both souls are naked at the time. That way their belt buckles don't get in the way of the merger.

He Said, She Said

Daisy Duck: "Donald gets a couple of beers in him and thinks he's Big Bird, if you know what I mean."

There is one more complication of sex. Because of sex, two people can engage in a fleeting act of passion that can lead to a second act that changes their lives forever. Experts call that second act "having a baby."

How did our early ancestors first figure out that having sex causes childbirth? After all, the two acts don't appear to be connected. The first is quite pleasant, and the second, as every mother knows only too well, involves excruciating pain when the father hits his thumb with a hammer while assembling the crib.

Considering how much we think about sex, today we don't know much more about it than those early ancestors did. Every so often scientists at a prestigious, research-oriented organization such as the Kinsey Institute sit around watching *Baywatch* until they get inspired to conduct an exhaustive study of the basic sexual knowledge of Americans. The scientists always come to the conclusion that, frankly, they would not want to drive out to Inspiration Point with *any* of us.

By the time the average women is twenty, she knows seventeen slang synonyms for the phrase "to have sex," but when asked to describe in physiological terms what happens when she and her mate engage in sex, she answers, "Well, usually I think about Fabio, and my husband hums 'The Battle Hymn of the Republic.'"

By the time the average man is twenty, he has spent a total of 342 hours staring intently at pictures of *Playboy* Playmates, but when shown a diagram of the female reproductive system, he mistakes it for a map of Manhattan. And believe me, you don't want to know what he identifies as Radio City Music Hall.

People know how to have sex but not what happens afterward.

So let's go through the steps with a typical couple. Okay. Dim the lights. A husband and a wife are minding their own business in their living room. He and she are each in their own little worlds. He is reading *Time*. She is reading *Newsweek*. Casually the man looks over at the woman. The woman looks back at the man. He puts down his *Time*. She puts down her *Newsweek*. In the bodies of the man and the woman, down at the hormones' union hall, the call goes out: "Hey, fellas, they're hiring!" The man flares one nostril. This means that he is aroused. If he flares *two* nostrils, it means that he is already halfway upstairs to the bedroom. She arches one eyebrow. This means that she, too, is aroused. If she arches *two* eyebrows, it means that she is surprised. Maybe she is surprised because they don't *have* an upstairs.

A few moments later, marriage has become a contact sport. The smoke alarm goes off, dogs bark, cats hiss, small children cry, furniture is broken. All too soon, the spent bodies of the man and woman have left Shroud of Turin–like sweat stains on the sheets.

The result of this liaison is that the man has contributed his sperm to the woman. Millions of sperm. It takes just one sperm to do the job, but, with federal government–like efficiency, millions are dispatched. Most of them just loaf a few hours in the cervix and then turn in a time card for a full day's work.

SEAMAN FIRST CLASS

Think of all those sperm as randy little sailors from the Seventh Fleet on shore leave. Think of the cervix as San Diego. To this scene the woman will contribute her egg. The egg slaps on a little lipstick, a spritz of Obsession, and moves provocatively down the fallopian tube toward her date with destiny. When the sperm see her, they whistle and hoot and holler and make rude kissing sounds. She is faintly flattered but mostly disgusted, but she also adores men in uniform and falls for the first sailor who treats her with respect and has sincere chromosomes. The egg and her chosen sperm have one date and only one date. This is "fertilization." Afterward, the sperm promises to stay in touch with the egg, but all he does is get a tattoo, write a few postcards, and go back to a bar to brag to his pals.

Meanwhile, back at the egg, cell division begins: One microscopic cell becomes two microscopic cells, two cells become four, four become eight, and so on until finally after a few months the woman must be lifted from a sitting position with a block and tackle.

You might think that the man's role in all this has ended. But no. He spends the last few months of gestation reassuring his wife that a woman whose silhouette can be mistaken for Alfred Hitchcock's still can be considered svelte.

Inside the woman, all those billions of dividing cells have become a fetus. From the fetus's point of view, it has it made.

Granted, its room is damp and the lighting is poor, but there are no chores and there is room service around the clock—food and beverage are piped in, even if the menu is limited.

Also, the fetus is not scolded for kicking, as it will be later in the outside world. In fact, kicking by a fetus is celebrated by the parents, who at such times often ask their friends to share their joy by feeling the woman's abdomen. Their friends always smile and agree to take part in this ritual, even though they secretly feel awkward, as if they've been asked to pet a huge matzo ball.

Also, thumb-sucking by the fetus is not discouraged. Little does the fetus know that thumb-sucking among older children is frowned upon and that thumb-sucking by adults will earn them a demerit on their job evaluation. Unless they work for the Hoover corporation, in which case they can call it "research and development."

Then, after nine months, at the most inconvenient time—usually during *Frasier*—nature tells the woman's body that it's time to rush to the hospital to sign lots of forms and releases. During all the red tape, when everyone is distracted, the baby is born.

After the baby goes home, it is placed in a spare bedroom that has been converted into a nursery at the same cost that it would take to convert Demi Moore to Dennis Rodman.

The baby soon begins to cry and leak from every available orifice. These two functions are right at the top of a baby's job description. Eventually all this crying and leaking triggers another biological response in the man and the woman: They hire a baby-sitter and get away for a weekend at the Hilton, where they take the phone off the hook, put a "do not disturb" sign on the doorknob, and relax by reading *Time* and *Newsweek*.

And the whole process starts all over again.

The Doctor Is In

It's time again to ask Dr. Romance:

Q. What is the difference between lust and love?

A. Lust is a flash fire; love is an eternal flame. And although both are pretty to look at, only lust requires asbestos underwear.

Q. Why do people kiss with their lips?

A. For two reasons: 1) because the lips are one of the most tactilely sensitive areas of the body surface, connected directly to that part of the brain that makes your toes curl and 2) because while two people are kissing with their lips, it greatly decreases the chance that they will say something stupid.

Q. Isn't passion one of the emotional parts of love?

A. Yes. Love is one part compatibility, one part compromise, and one part passion.

Q. What if your husband hasn't touched you since early in the Truman administration?

A. Dr. Romance did not say that those are *equal* parts.

Q. Should sex be approached with caution, reserve, and deliberation?

A. Yes. Remember that fools rush in where angels fear to tread. However, also remember that fools who rush in get the best parking spaces.

CHAPTER Four

Women: I Am Woman, Hear Me Taupe

REMEMBER THOSE science fiction movies of the '50s and '60s? There was always a scene in which the space alien or the monster appeared suddenly, causing the stars and hundreds of extras to flee in panic. And among those fleeing there was always a pretty young woman who fell down and twisted her ankle and was rendered helpless. Then she was carried off screaming to the swamp by the Creature from the Black Lagoon, who was in a foul mood because his rubber costume was hot and chafing and not anatomically correct.

No more. Today's woman is not afraid of monsters. After all, she has stood up to her boss, her ex-husband, and that snotty little man down at the bank.

For generations woman was expected to get a high school diploma, a husband, and morning sickness, preferably in that order.

No more. Today's woman has greater expectations. This is her century. Woman has come out of the kitchen and out of the closet, taken off her apron and her wedding band, burned her bra and her meat loaf. She has found that anything that a man can do, a woman can do, *and* while retaining water.

With all the changes happening in the wonderful world of women, these days it's difficult for us to generalize about woman. But if we didn't, this chapter would be about forty

words long. So here we go: Consider this scenario—you are home alone late at night. Your doorbell rings. You get out of bed, put on your robe and slippers, look out the peephole, and see a strange man on your porch. You are wary, if not downright frightened, and do not open the door.

Now consider this scenario—you are home alone late at night. Your doorbell rings. You get out of bed, put on your robe and slippers, look out the peephole, and see a strange woman on your porch. You open the door.

Why do you fear the man but not the woman? Because although the man might rob you, harm you, or even kill you, the worst that the woman might do to you is point out that your robe clashes with your slippers.

Yes, women are less aggressive and violent than men. This is because women suffer from a deficiency of testosterone—the male hormone. In laboratory studies, women who are given doses of testosterone develop a sudden urge to get into a barroom brawl, go to a tractor pull, and use the word *hooters*.

In place of testosterone, women have estrogen. Estrogen is the hormone that controls women's reproductive cycles, produces their female physical characteristics, and gives them the uncanny ability to walk into a bar containing a hundred men and fall for the one man who has a wife, two children, and a mother who also happens to be the bouncer.

RED, WHITE, AND BALMY BAHAMA BLUE

Women are sensitive organisms, very in touch with their surroundings. They can smell dust. They can hear dirt.

Women also are very visual, attuned to color. They can distinguish forty-three shades of gray. They speak a complex secret language of color. They know fifty-seven adjectives to modify "blue." A woman can go into a store and say, "I want something in Balmy Bahama blue with a hint of mint," and the saleswoman will know *exactly* what she means!

The names that women give to colors are never simple. There is no such color as "just plain white." No, there's Navajo white or Eggshell white or The Sole of Isadora Duncan's Left Foot on a Warm Spring Evening white.

Women are conversant about colors that have prissy names such as *mauve* and *puce* and *taupe*. Just what is *taupe* anyway? A man can tell you what *taupe* is: *Taupe* is a word that women made up to make men feel stupid and unsophisticated. That's the real reason why male athletes are reluctant to allow female reporters in their locker rooms—they're afraid that the women will shout "Taupe!"

Women know which colors make people look their best. Women talk easily about the color of one thing bringing out a color in another thing that the first thing is near. "See how this skirt brings out the blue in this blouse?" A woman would see it instantly. A man would ask, "Now this one is the skirt, right?"

When moving into a house and decorating it, a woman will want to coordinate colors, pick the perfect wallpaper, the perfect furniture, matching drapes, pillow shams, the right frames for pictures. To a man, unless the house is actually on fire when he moves in, it will be fine just as it is.

To men all this fuss about color seems so pointless. To them, in the cosmic scheme of things color is not important in the same way that, for example, mag wheels are.

Women are at ease with highly technical clothing terms, such as "size." They know how to select clothes that make them look thinner or taller, that accent their eyes, that draw attention away from their ankles. They can take a simple accessory like a scarf and make it serve thirty-seven different fashion purposes. Thirty-eight if you count wearing it as a scarf.

He Said, She Said

Lord Godiva: "Gee, I guess that when she told me she didn't have a thing to wear, she wasn't exaggerating."

BETTY JEAN, THE GYPSY QUEEN

Woman has her contradictions, her share of ambivalence.

She may want to be considered a person first and a woman

second; she may want the respect and all the rights that her gender has been denied throughout history; she may want equal pay for equal hyperacidity. But she also wants romance. She wants love to be something soulful and magical, a kind of alchemy that transmutes the straw of her mundane existence into the gold of moonlight, violins, and rose petals. But although she dreams of a handsome knight on a white horse, she'll be darned if she's going to polish his armor and sweep the stable.

She may tell herself that she wants a man who is sensitive, gentle, and intelligent. But while driving past a biker bar she may find herself staring at a menacing Hell's Angel and wanting to jump onto the back of his Harley and roar off with him to live the life of a gypsy queen: living and loving on the edge, wearing denim and leather, defying conventions and the law. Just as long as they steal a TV once in a while so that she can get caught up on *Days of Our Lives*.

She may want to be valued for her mind, she may not want men to see her as a sex object. But she also didn't buy that two-hundred-dollar black miniskirt to show off her SAT scores.

Her home and physical grooming—makeup, dress, hair, accessories—may be immaculate. But her purse may be a yawning black hole that over the years has sucked in receipts, ticket stubs, matchbooks, a family of combs and brushes, earrings, dribs and drabs of makeup carbon-dated at 1972, gum wrappers, keys for a car she sold during the Carter administration, half-eaten bars of candy, slips of paper containing phone numbers and addresses, homework assignments from high school, Jimmy Hoffa, Ambrose Bierce, and Amelia Earhart requesting permission to land.

Her Vision of What Heaven Will Be Like

☛ In heaven, cellulite is considered attractive.

☛ Angels have no visible panty lines.

☛ Finds out that her ex-husband went the other way.

☛ James Dean lets her drive his car.

☛ Down on Earth, every time a microwave oven rings, an angel gets her wings.

☛ Not only is God a woman, but She, too, doesn't think that the Three Stooges are funny.

☛ It takes her just one kiss to change Rock Hudson's mind.

☛ She beats Bobby Riggs in straight sets.

☛ Eleanor Roosevelt is the line judge.

☛ She has the figure she had at twenty-two.

☛ She has the earning power she had at thirty-two.

☛ She has the smarts she had at forty-two.

☛ She has the teenage cabana boy she had at fifty-two.

☛ Men are expected to clean their own fish.

☛ JFK hits on her.

☛ LBJ doesn't hit on her.

☛ In heaven, chocolate is health food.

☛ Equal pay for equal harp playing.

☛ She is invited to a slumber party by pioneer feminists Elizabeth Cady Stanton, Susan B. Anthony, and Lucretia Mott.

☛ The four of them stay up all night painting each other's toenails and making crank calls to the Playboy Mansion.

A woman has a secure and an insecure side. When she is feeling secure, her posture is statuesque, her voice is firm.

She practically glows—streetlights switch off as she walks under them. As she walks, her hips activate seismographs, registering 6.4—capable of causing cups to fall from shelves and male drivers to swerve onto the sidewalk. She makes decisions quickly and confidently.

When she is feeling insecure, her "little ol' me" side emerges. She feels unattractive, overweight, frumpy. She is more easily influenced than at other times. When she walks onto a car lot, salesmen can sense her insecurity and dust off the AMC Pacer that they keep at the back of the lot for such occasions. She becomes indecisive. At lunch, she can't decide between soup and salad. She finally resorts to flipping a coin. But she can't decide between a nickel and a dime.

THE BONES OF CONTENTION

Despite her advances this century, woman faces many challenges. Some of these challenges are minor; some of these challenges are men.

Gender-based roles persist to hold her back. The glass ceiling has cracked but not collapsed. Some occupations are slow to accept her. Domestic stereotypes linger. Just how did gender-based roles begin anyway? Anthropologists theorize that women got mired in their traditional roles by default. For millions of years primitive men and women had lived in equality, living off berries and raw meat. They threw the bones onto the floor of their cave. Then one day, a primitive man woke up early and was hungry for steak. So he sneaked out of the cave to kill a mastodon and discover fire.

It's a wonder he didn't wake his primitive woman, rattling all those bones as he waded to the front of the cave. With him out of the cave all day, someone had to care for the children and sweep out all those bones. The bones were becoming so high that some of the shorter children had not been seen in several days. Sometimes in a far corner of the cave, the bones would rattle and you'd hear a muffled "Mommy?"

He Said, She Said

Mr. Crocker: "For God's sake, Betty, can't we have pie just once?!"

Soon these gender roles were a tradition, and others were founded on them. Man left the cave to hunt. Woman stayed home with the bones. When a primitive woman had the temerity to suggest to her mate that he help around the cave, he would look up from his easy chair and reply:

"Can't right now, Honey. I'm busy evolving."

WHAT'S A WOMAN TO DO, DAD?

Another challenge that a woman faces is the female body. She first becomes aware of her body during puberty with her monthly cycle, which her mother tells her is just nature's way of reminding her how lucky she is to be a woman. She is unconvinced, and suspects that a written reminder would have been sufficient.

She soon discovers that a woman's body is very complex. Her reproductive system—apparently designed by Rube Goldberg—consists of various solenoids, toggle switches, levers, chutes and ladders, valves, funnels, receptacles, and several yards of tubing. If it were made of copper, it could be used as a still.

But when you think about it, any system that can produce a real live human baby in just nine months using just water, hydrogen, oxygen, carbon, and a splash of Giorgio *has* to be complex. It has to have a lot of complex doodads in there. And those doodads can get out of whack. So a woman has to see her doctor often. At least that's what her doctor tells her. Her doctor gives her a thorough examination and renders a detailed diagnosis: "It is my professional medical opinion, based on years of training and practice, that your doodad is out of whack."

Keeping such a complex system fit as a fiddle is expensive for women. One in seven Mercedes-Benzes on the road today was paid for by a woman's doodad.

Things That Women Most Want to Be Reincarnated As

☛ A ballerina
☛ A leopard
☛ Alan Jackson's guitar pick
☛ George Clooney's Batman tights
☛ Sheena, queen of the jungle
☛ Sheena, queen of *any*thing

Health care is a part of life for women. Putting their body in the care of others is routine. They get their ears pierced, they get bikini-waxed, they see their doctors for intimate examinations that a man would submit to only after 1. a general anesthetic; and 2. an engagement ring.

Women also go through labor. Hours of labor. Days of labor. Not that a woman minds, not that she harbors any resentment toward her children for putting her through morning sickness and labor and stretch marks. But years later, she does chuckle gleefully as she shows photos of her children's toilet training to each of their dates.

Some of woman's challenges are more subtle. For example, she must fight the temptation to meet the physical standard set by centerfold women, with their button noses and cigar-band waists and breasts that have to be kept in dirigible hangars. The way that a woman perceives her physical appearance affects her self-esteem. And she seldom is satisfied with her appearance, seldom sees herself as others see her. In reality she may look like a goddess—she may have a face like Aphrodite; she may have a voluptuous figure that could trigger armed conflict in a Quaker village.

But she sees her physical appearance as flawed. She hates her thighs. "I can feel fat cells from all over my body taking early retirement and moving to my thighs. My thighs are the Florida of my body."

She hates her hair. "Look at this tangle. I feel like Medusa. I should get my hair done by a herpetologist!"

She hates her bottom. "Like the universe, my rear is expanding, getting ever larger. The difference is that the universe just has to drift through infinity; my rear has to fit into size-twelve jeans."

Mother Goose Update

Little Miss Muffet sat on a tuffet,
Eating her curds and whey.
Along came a spider and sat down beside her
And frightened Miss Muffet away.

MUFFETVILLE—"I owe my life to that spider," Ms. Muffet said as she proudly modeled a size-four dress.

"This is the new me. The new, thin me. I've lost 180 pounds and nine dress sizes. I am also down to a size-forty-four tuffet.

"See," she explained, "when that spider—God bless him—sat down beside me, I was so frightened that I ran away. Well, I say 'ran.' 'Waddled' is closer to the truth. I had gotten so fat from eating curds and whey that I weighed almost three hundred pounds. Do you know how fattening curds and whey are?! I got so heavy that it affected my social life. My self-esteem was low. I was too insecure to date. I stayed home watching the Home Shopping Network. And I couldn't stop eating curds and whey. The fatter I got, the more depressed I got, and the more I ate to console myself.

"Anyway, as I ran from that spider I was out of breath after fifty feet. Then I fell down, and I rolled another fifty. After I came to a stop, as I lay there gasping, I thought I was dying. My entire pantry passed before my eyes. I vowed that if I lived, I would lose that weight and keep it off.

"And I have. Here's my secret: Every time I am tempted to eat something fattening, I have that spider sit down beside me and frighten me. I call it my 'Eight Legs to a Thinner You Diet.' And it works. Fear is a powerful motivator.

"I just wish that spider had sat down beside me as I was saying 'I do' to my first husband."

DURESS FOR SUCCESS

Women, more than men, have been affected by the vagaries of fashion. Four hundred years ago, during Rubens's time, an ample female figure was fashionable. Thin women were *déclassé.* Sometimes two thin women would get into the same dress together to pass as one chunky woman. And it worked:

"Va va voom! Dig that chunky chick over there!"

"You mean the one with four legs?"

Three hundred years later, women laced themselves into corsets whose ribs were made of whalebone. Many a woman came home from a party and beached herself on the settee. Then, during the Roaring Twenties, curves and bosoms were deemphasized. The ideal woman's figure was mannish. That's why the Twenties were called "Roaring"—women went around roaring, "We want our bosoms back!"

Today woman wears an assortment of foundations to achieve the current "look." She wears a slip or half-slip, panties, pantyhose, and possibly, for the full-figured masochist, a girdle. She may wear a bra so sturdy that it not only lifts and separates but also can withstand a head-on collision of fifteen miles per hour. This collection of undergarments encases her. She leaves the house each day feeling like a sausage with eyeliner.

At the end of the day, when she undresses and gets out of harness, telltale red creases on bare skin around hips, chest, and back show where the elastic of straps and waistbands has dug in, where buckles and belts have bitten, where snaps, brads, wires, and shoes with pointed toes have pinched. She looks as if she has been mugged by a lobster.

Just to see how the other half lives, every man—and especially those men who design women's clothes—should be required to wear bra, girdle, pantyhose, high heels—the whole female kit and caboodle ("Do you have this caboodle in a size thirty-four?") for two weeks.

One week if he seems to be enjoying it a bit too much.

Not only are such women's undergarments cruel and unusual, they also are expensive. Oddly, the larger the underwear is, the less it costs. Big, billowy underwear—the kind that can be used as a drag chute for the space shuttle—is so inexpensive that many gas stations give away pairs as a premium with a ten-gallon fill-up. Thus the price scale for women's undergarments is the same as that for corn: Those tiny ears of baby corn cost much more than the larger, standard ears. The difference is that it is not considered sexy for a woman to wear vegetables beneath an evening gown.

Indications That There's Trouble in Paradise

☞ Your spouse uses your marriage license as a paper towel.

☞ You see a strange pair of shoes under your bed.

☞ You see a strange pair of feet under your bed.

☞ At a restaurant, your spouse leaves his wedding band on the table as a tip.

☞ Your mate takes a job as a Domino's deliverer, volunteers for a suicide mission.

☞ She superglues shut the zipper on all your slacks.

☞ Your mate kisses with eyes open, drives with eyes closed.

☞ Spouse nails self into a big crate, addresses it to "Anywhere but here."

☞ She puts all her spare change into a big jar labeled "HUNK."

☞ You find him idly spelling out "R-E-N-O" in his alphabet soup.

☞ Spouse's favorite Internet Web page address is "http://www.annul.com."

☞ During sex, your mate works a crossword puzzle.

☞ During the climax of sex, your mate mutters, "Six-letter word for dull."

OH, WOE, WOE IS WOMAN?

Whereas men feel the stress of asking women out, women feel the stress of being asked out by men. After all, any woman, without warning, may be asked out by any man, no matter where on the food chain he falls. He might be a colleague. He might be a friend who has misinterpreted a word or a look. He might be married. He might be a total stranger who walks up to her in a bar and asks her out based on nothing more than the fact that he just spilled beer down her blouse. In high school, he may have been voted most likely to die in a hail of gunfire. He may have a tattoo that reads "begat and be gone." He may have bad teeth, and when he smiles (which is *much* too often) his mouth may look like a bowl of mixed nuts. She can't help but notice that his wisdom cashews are coming in.

But when such men ask a woman out, she has to handle them all. If she is not interested in the man, at the most she must be gracious and tactful; at the least she must be firm yet self-protecting. On the other hand, if she is interested in the man, she must appear receptive yet cool while secretly her internal organs are exchanging "high fives."

Words That Women Hate to Hear

- ☞ "Put your feet in the stirrups."
- ☞ "We don't have it in a larger size."
- ☞ "Do you mind if my mother comes along with us?"

☞ "Now don't take this the wrong way…"

☞ "Want a chaw of my Redman?"

☞ "I don't know how to thank you. You've made me realize that I don't feel comfortable with heterosexuality."

Woman is at last coming into her own sexually. She is finding that it's OK to have a libido and to direct it at more than just romance novels. She is finding that it's OK these days for a woman to make the first move. Still, at some point she expects the man to take the hint and do his share. For example, if a woman presses herself against a man, he is expected to put his arm around her. If a woman puts her head on the man's shoulder, he is expected to kiss her. If she takes off all her clothes and anoints her body with peanut butter, he is expected to supply the grape jelly.

But some things never change. One of the biggest complaints that single women have about men is that at the end of what the woman perceived to be a very successful date, the man promises: "I had a really nice time. I'll call you soon." And he doesn't. Days go by. Then weeks. The seasons change. Her psoriasis clears up. Nothing. And each time that the phone doesn't ring, she knows that's him. She can hear him out there somewhere, not dialing.

She could understand if the evening had been a bomb. In fact, then she would *hope* that he wouldn't call soon. But because the evening seemed to go so well, the woman is puzzled. She begins to doubt her own perceptions. Did she mishear him? Did she miss some terrible social gaffe? Did she imagine the entire date? No, it really happened. She has a symphony program, an after-dinner mint, and a hickey as proof.

And he seemed to have a good time and to enjoy her company. They laughed, they talked. There were no stretches of awkward "God, this date is death. When will it end?" silence.

She reviews the evening in her head, much as how football teams watch the film of a game afterward: "Okay, here we are having dinner. We're talking easily. He's making me laugh. I'm making him laugh. I don't see any spinach between my teeth. And here we are dancing later. We move together okay. He's not holding me like I might stain his clothes."

So where did he go? To answer this question, recently scientists tagged single men with electronic devices and tracked them after they promised to "call you soon" at the end of a date. It was discovered that they all go to Montana. There they establish communities and contract various services from each other. Then, when payment is due, they promise each other, "The check's in the mail."

Yes, by the time a woman is thirty, she has had so many bad experiences in love that she dreams of a program similar to the federal witness protection program that would relocate victims of bad dates and bad relationships to another city and give them a new life: a new look, a new identity, a new dating pool, a new hope. Personally, she'd like to be relocated to some nice town in a primitive tropical country where the ratio of men to women is twenty to one and she runs the only combination bait shop/malaria clinic in town.

Heck, she tells herself after she's started her new life, she'd even go out with the Creature from the Black Lagoon. He'd probably be a sweet guy if someone just decorated his lagoon for him. Taupe sounds nice.

Men: He-Man, Hee-Haw

EVENTUALLY A WOMAN will have to deal with a man, be it her father, brother, husband, son, date, or auto mechanic. This means that he is going to raise her, razz her, make her pregnant, bring a frog into her kitchen, try to kiss her, or tell her that "your hydraulic mezzoconfabulator is preigniting your catalytic transferentializer, little lady."

With all these men around, no wonder women wish that they knew how to understand and live in harmony with them. Or at least how to strangle them without breaking a fingernail.

Just who is this big lug we call "man" anyway? Well, man is just like other people, only a little more confused. He is Contradiction with an Adam's apple; he is Conflict in argyle socks. He is a grab bag of opposites: good and evil, method and madness, black and white (you'll find the black on your best hand towels after he works on the car).

Remember: This is the gender that gave us Disneyland and Jonestown, hula hoops and Hiroshima, Mister Rogers and Jolly Rogers.

A man may be enlightened and chauvinistic, easygoing and domineering, sometimes all in the same interoffice memo.

He may take his car to a mechanic for a tune-up every six months but never take himself to the doctor. Not going to a doctor is one of those things that men are inexplicably proud of, like being able to spit for distance or eat nineteen hot dogs. "Ah ain't been to no doctor in nigh on to twenty year," boasts the man with a growth on his neck so large that airlines make him buy an extra ticket for it.

A man will willingly inflict pain on himself with sports, exercise, and hobbies. But let a nurse try to prick his finger, and suddenly he's a two-year-old with five o'clock shadow.

He Said, She Said

Mr. Nightingale: "Florence is never home anymore. You know? She's always off at some hospital or disaster scene. I don't see how she does it. There's all that red, viscous blood gushing and the smell of rubbing alcohol and those long needles and...and...ooooooo" (thud).

The same man who is adept in his workshop may be at a total loss in the kitchen. He doesn't know an eggbeater from an egg timer. Measurements like "Tbs." and "Tsp." intimidate him. His culinary skill is limited to making a personal-size planetarium by inverting a colander over his head and looking up at the kitchen light ("Look—is that Ursa Major or last night's spaghetti?").

A man will devote six years to restoring a car and thirty seconds to dressing for a date. The clothes he chooses may look like a TV test pattern with cuffs.

He may relate to a woman in opposite ways. When he is insecure, he slouches, hides his hands in his pockets, twists the toe of his Hush Puppy in the ground, looks her squarely in the chin, and mumbles: "You wouldn't want to go out with me, would you?"

Ah, but when he is secure, he exudes confidence from every pore. He stands several centimeters taller, his shoulders are several degrees squarer. His stride becomes a swagger; his nostrils flare roguishly. He looks her squarely in the eye and says, in a tone that is as much command as invitation: "You. Me. Tonight. Ecstasy. Be there."

He then gives her the same masterful look that Alexander the Great gave India.

He leaves her breathless and strangely yearning for curry powder.

THE EMPIRE STATE BABY

It has been said that man—denied woman's ability to procreate—creates. In his quest for immortality he has written novels, painted paintings, sculpted statues, built skyscrapers, bridges, and dams. He has given birth to such creations as gunpowder, movable type, and the wheel. Soon we had heavily armed bookmobiles.

Such creations are men's children. The difference between these children and the kind that women have is that the

Golden Gate Bridge won't give you stretch marks, and the *Mona Lisa* won't phone you at 2 A.M. to tell you that she just wrecked the family car.

This drive to create makes man the ultimate do-it-your-selfer. He wants to fix his car, repair his home, even try to solve his emotional problems without seeking help from others. He defines himself by what he does, by what he achieves and creates with his mind or his hands. After he dies, he stands before St. Peter and hands him his college transcript, his résumé, and snapshots of every bookcase and deck he ever built.

And St. Peter, being a guy, understands perfectly and compliments him on his miter cuts.

Man gets a real sense of achievement from spending only seven hours of labor and $124 in materials to build something that he could have bought for less than $30.

So man surrounds himself with hardware: tools and stuff. Men love stuff: nuts, bolts, screws, nails, cotter pins, pop rivets, thingamabobs, doohickeys. Stuff has so much potential. With stuff, man can do so much, well, stuff. He fills jars and cans with hard, shiny, machined metal bits of stuff and keeps them in neat rows on workshop shelves. He may have inherited some from his father. In turn, he hands them down, like heirlooms, to his own son: "To my three daughters I leave $100,000 each. And to my son, the joy of my life, I leave my coffee can full of wing nuts."

He prowls home improvement centers fondling the tools. Routers and drills and saws, oh, my! As he handles a saw, he fantasizes about the wondrous projects he could create with it, the male friends he could impress, the fingers he could lose, enabling him to stay home on sick leave and watch *Oprah*.

He lines the walls of his garage with tools, neatly arranged on Peg Board. On weekends he straps on a tool belt bristling with manly hammers and pliers and wrenches and feels down-right adequate. Tools give man the impression that he has control of something. He thinks: "I might not be able to control my teenagers, my computer, my career, or my blood pressure, but by God and Bob Vila I can control my cordless drill. Just as soon as my teenagers finish using it to pierce their ears."

Words That Men Hate to Hear

- ☛ "The doctor will see you now."
- ☛ "Now don't take this the wrong way…"
- ☛ "Can't we be just friends?"
- ☛ "I've been seeing another man."
- ☛ "I've been seeing another woman."
- ☛ "Uh, weren't you wearing a condom when we started?"

Of course, with his mind so preoccupied with writing novels, building skyscrapers, sculpting statues, and such, man can be a bit lax in other areas of his life:

When he blows his nose, trombones in heat show up outside the window. He may or may not use a handkerchief.

He may get his hair cut by positioning himself one inch under a ceiling fan and then standing on tiptoes.

He may be the major distributor of methane for the tri-state area.

He may eat all his meals over the sink.

If shipwrecked, he could live for days by sucking the stains on his tie.

His kitchen may have enough dirt in it to grow crops.

He may own a pair of novelty briefs that bear the words *Home of the Whopper*.

This description is, of course, a composite. There is probably no one man who has all these characteristics. But if there is, rest assured that your daughter will find him.

TESTOSTERONE: NATURE'S MOLOTOV COCKTAIL

Not everything that man creates is good. Man creates most of the wars, most of the violent crimes, and most of the shoving in line to get nachos at the ball game. Man will resort to fists, knives, or ballistic missiles over most anything: a word spoken in anger, a "dirty" look, a woman, a contest of skill, greed.

The Falklands War began when the men of England and the men of Argentina disputed ownership of a scattering of rocky, barren islands. England and Argentina each claimed that the islands belonged to the other country.

World War II began when Hitler invaded Poland in 1939, telling Poland that he had just come to read the meter.

Why are men so aggressive? Researcher Richard Estes studied male wildebeests in Africa and concluded that testosterone produces aggression in men. And what are men but wildebeests in boxer shorts?

Testosterone is the male sex hormone that also triggers in a man such male characteristics as upper-body mass, facial hair, deep voice, and the tendency to pick his nose at red lights.

Under chemical analysis, testosterone is found to be powerful stuff, containing water, carbon, nitroglycerin, kerosene, Budweiser, seltzer, Tabasco, a splash of Old Spice, and just a trace of Jack's Secret Sauce.

Testosterone is what makes a male a male. It's also what makes many men need to prove their maleness by fighting and macho posturing. And yet their maleness is written right there on their birth certificate on Day One. Under "sex" there is a big "M" for "male." The world would be a far quieter place if men proved their manhood by just whipping out their birth certificates and saying, "Hey, punk. See that 'M'?"

Of course, that would probably only lead to a knife fight over whose "M" is bigger.

Aggression in men is nothing new. Another researcher, Konrad Lorenz, said aggression in men began when men were primitive providers-protectors, when we had to fend off wild animals and stalk fleet-footed wild game for food. But need for such aggression is anachronistic today. Modern man does not need to protect his 3-2-2 brick cave against saber-toothed tigers, and even the swiftest TV dinner can't run very fast.

Yet testosterone continues to trigger aggression. Bad, bad hormone. Ah, but testosterone also triggers the sex drive. Nice, nice hormone. Thus the same hormone that triggers violent, aggressive impulses that sometimes threaten the human race *also* triggers sexual urges, ensuring perpetuation of the human race. This is like putting the brakes and the accelerator on the same pedal. Yes, once again Mother Nature has given us a tradeoff: The same hormone that makes a man want to make love with the Swedish Bikini Team all weekend also makes him want to get up on Monday morning and bomb Stockholm.

RBIs, PATs, AND TKOs

Fortunately, man channels some of his aggression into socially acceptable competition—sports. A man takes his sports seriously, leading many a woman to ask:

"Why is it that a man can remain faithful to the same sports team his entire life but can't remain faithful to the same woman for ten years?"

"Why is it that he can't remember our anniversary or my birthday, but he can remember arcane sports statistics of men with names like 'Three Finger' Brown, 'Too Tall' Jones, and 'Boom Boom' Mancini?"

"And did he *have* to name our first child after 'Goose' Gossage? She has to live with that the rest of her life."

He Said, She Said

Mrs. Hansel: "Sure, Hansel could remember to leave behind a trail of bread crumbs, but could he ever remember Valentine's Day?"

THE GOOD DYE YOUNG

Despite men's physical strength, they don't live as long as women do. This is partly because many of men's gender-based roles are stressful. Perhaps most stressful of all, men are expected to ask women out on dates. Aaaaaaaeeeeeeeee! The anxiety of preparing for this social death plunge will turn a man's hair gray and shorten his life quicker than anything else. The anxiety is understandable, considering that men regard women as mysterious, wondrous creatures with special powers: the power to prepare meals that don't include Velveeta as the main course, the power to paralyze a 200-pound man with a flash of bare midriff at fifty paces, the power to walk into a room and notice a stain on a sofa when a man would not even notice the sofa.

And scariest of all: the power to say "no."

The fear of rejection grips a man as he prepares to call a woman to ask her out. He writes a script to follow. He makes practice calls to the time and temperature recording. Then (gulp) he makes The Call. By the time the woman answers, his throat is so constricted with fear that he can make only sputtering, gurgling noises. The woman listens to these noises a few moments and then shouts to her cappuccino machine: "It's for you."

Things That Men Most Want to Be Reincarnated As

- A rogue wolf
- A Triple Crown winner put out to stud
- Albert Belle's bat
- Pamela Anderson Lee's loofah sponge

Man's Idea of What Heaven Will Be Like

- He is assigned a cloud next to Jayne Mansfield's.
- Hendrix asks him if he wants to jam.
- Hot pants are still in fashion.
- It rains beer and snows pretzels.
- He has a hairline and a waistline again.
- Free HBO.
- He doesn't have to get to the office until ten.
- Marilyn Monroe returns his phone calls.
- He gets to drink beer with Babe Ruth until both throw up.
- They both throw up on his high school PE teacher.
- Men are required to leave their prostates at the Pearly Gates.
- His lawn is mowed by Charlemagne.

- ☞ Poker every Friday night. God brings the dip.
- ☞ John Wayne calls him "Sir."
- ☞ George Halas asks him to quarterback heaven's football team.
- ☞ He leads the team to victory over hell's team in the annual Soul Bowl.

There are other threats to the longevity of man. Man is expected to do things that expose him to injury. Such as wars. Man must fight in them and risk being promoted to the rank of dead.

And hunting. Men are expected to want to hunt, to go out into the woods with an arsenal of rifles, bullets, scopes, knives, and binoculars. The Persian Gulf War would have been over in about twenty minutes if Iraq had been invaded by Allied deer hunters.

Man is expected to want to fish. A man who doesn't care for fishing may even force himself to go, afraid that if he doesn't, all his male friends who do fish will break into his home, pull down his Dockers, and spank him with a large trout.

Man is expected to be strong and silent, to hold in his emotions, to suffer in silence. This suppression is stressful. Every once in a while, man would like to let loose and scream: "Ouuuuuch! Fellas, that trout *hurts*!"

Of course, not all men enjoy these stereotypical male things. Not all men get the hang of spitting and cussing. Or learn to like beer. Or carry a pocketknife. They don't hunt or fish. The only prey they stalk for food are Tater Tots in the supermarket freezer section. And even then, they worry that the Taters leave behind a family.

Mother Goose Update

Jack and Jill went up the hill,
to fetch a pail of water;
Jack fell down and broke his crown
And Jill came tumbling after.

HILLSDALE—"Funny how something so commonplace can change your life," Jill said, looking fondly at the now-rusting old pail that was the beginning of it all so many years ago.

"Jack was never the same after he broke his crown. The doctors examined him and said he'd never be quite 'right.' We were just childhood friends at the time of the accident. But after the accident, our friendship grew into something more. Jack needed me. I felt guilty because I was not seriously injured but he was. Our friendship grew into love. At least I know I love Jack. And I think Jack loves me, in his own way. But sometimes his mind wanders. When it does, he relives World War I. Then he thinks I am Captain von Richtofen, and he chases me around the house shouting, 'Death to the Hun!'"

Jill keeps the pail in a place of honor on the mantel in their cottage.

"We don't go up the hill for water anymore," she said. "We have Sparkletts deliver to our home now. But I have to keep Jack away from the delivery man. Jack is convinced that the guy is Kaiser Wilhelm."

Man also is expected to perform certain domestic duties. He is the one who must go into the bathroom to kill a spider the size of a sumo wrestler, get a stubborn cap off a ketchup bottle, and, when his wife hears an intruder downstairs in the night, go down and investigate armed only with a rolled-up *TV Guide*. As he creeps downstairs, he wishes he hadn't killed that big bathroom spider—he could have sent *it* down to hit the intruder with that ketchup bottle.

DESTINATION: DISCOMFORT

Being goal-oriented, man often displays a single-minded dedication to task. Especially when driving long distances. Just ask his family. First he has the kids nail his hands to the steering wheel. Then he has his wife nail his right foot to the gas pedal. Then they're off, and Dad won't stop again except for gas until he reaches his destination. No food stops. No rest stops. Damn the bladders, full speed ahead!

Yes, a road map, a tank of gas, and a catheter, and man is ready to roll. On a trip across country, if he passes within sixty miles of the Grand Canyon on the way to somewhere else, he refuses to make that short detour to splendor. "If God had intended people to visit the Grand Canyon," Dad says, "He would have built it on the interstate."

He Said, She Said

Mrs. Lewis and Mrs. Clark: "Those two guys traveled four thousand miles to get from the Missouri River to Oregon. You know why? Because they were lost most of the time! But would they ever stop to ask directions? Hah! Too bad they didn't, because when they left home, their original destination was the 7-Eleven eight blocks away!"

Man, of course, has a thing about cars. A woman is apt to see her car as a means to an end. To a man, his car is an end in itself. It might be a rolling landfill to others, but to him it is a delicate treasure, a Faberge Pinto.

Men love their cars, part with them reluctantly. Every man remembers his first car, and most remember it fondly, no matter how cantankerous it was. Here is an open letter from one middle-aged man to a '51 Pontiac, wherever it may be:

SPUTTERING DOWN MEMORY LANE

We never forget the big firsts in our life, do we? And you were my first car, oh, Pontiac of my past. I would go on to own more than a dozen cars over the years. But through them

all, you left a soft spot in my heart, a warm spot in my memories, and an oil spot in my parents' driveway.

We were both fifteen when we met. You were big and heavy, with sixteen-inch tires, a long hood covering a flat-head straight-eight engine, and a cavernous trunk that I sublet to a family of gypsies. With your metal windshield visor and grille of chrome teeth, yours was a stern visage. But to this teenage boy, you were a madonna in mud flaps, a venus in Valvoline.

It's an American tradition to marry young boys to old cars. And from the beginning, ours was a marriage of inconvenience.

I paid fifty dollars for you in 1965, remember? And during the daylight hours, you were worth every dollar. During the day, I could count on you to get me to school, to a summer job, to baseball practice. But you apparently belonged to some fringe auto religion that didn't believe in doing work after dark. You would never start at night. And with that sixth sense that is standard equipment on clunkers such as you, you *knew* when I really needed you to start in the worst way. This was usually about 11:52 P.M. after the second feature at the drive-in. My date had to be home by midnight. If she was late, her father would put his arm around my shoulder, nod his head understandingly and, in a fatherly way, tie my throat into a granny knot.

This would be a definite handicap during my final exam in speech class.

Every Friday and Saturday night at 11:52 at the drive-in, I would clench my teeth, close my eyes, and push the starter button, only to hear the most dreaded, most sickening, most disgusting nonintestinal sound in all the world:

"RRRRRrrrrRRRRrrrRRRRRrrrr...rrrr...rrr...rr..."

And the rest, as Hamlet said when his Yugo wouldn't start, was silence.

Then I'd get out and rush over to the car parked next to mine and urgently knock on a fogged front window. "Oh, *there* you are," I'd say as some dreamy-eyed fellow teen rolled down the *back* window. As he got out of his car to get his jumper cables, he'd make a sullen "you owe me *big*" growling noise not unlike yours:

"RRRRRrrrrRRRRrrrRRRRRrrrr...rrrr...rr..."

But he'd give me a battery boost, you'd fire right up in a belch of black smoke, and I wouldn't have to ask the gypsies to get out of the trunk and push.

I did everything I could to make you reliable. I brought you offerings: a new battery, starter, solenoid, voltage regulator, generator. I took you to a mechanic. He suggested a faith healer. Obediently, I took you to a faith healer. He suggested that I drive you through the carwash at Lourdes.

Then, predictably, I resorted to a favorite superstition of teenage male owners of marginal cars: I prettied you up. The reasoning apparently is: If I lavish enough devotion on my car, it will return my devotion.

So I put whitewall tires on your wheels. I put new covers on your seats. I washed you, anointed you with Turtle Wax.

Then I drove you back to the drive-in. Only to hear:

"RRRRRrrrrRRRRrrrRRRRRrrrr...rrrr...rr..."

I added more chrome to you. Floor mats. Steering wheel cover. Then back to the drive-in:

"RRRRRrrrrRRRRrrrRRRRRrrrr...rrrr...rr..."

And so it went all that summer of '65 until, finally, in a weak moment of frustration, I threw you over for that cute little MG. But I cried as we parted. Did you ever forgive me? I've often wondered what became of you. You probably rolled out your last miles as someone's "second car." But after that, I hope, you were crushed and recycled to live again, perhaps reincarnated as thousands of tin cans.

In fact, I think of you each time I see a tin can. And who knows, maybe we'll meet again. If some night around 11:52, I try to open a can of peas or carrots, only to hear my electric can opener go:

"RRRRRrrrrRRRRRrrrRRRRRrrrr...rrrr...rrr...rr..."

I'll know that we're together again.

CHAPTER

Six

Dating: The Single File

IN THE GREAT amusement park of life, most of us would prefer to spend all of our time sailing dreamily through the tunnel of love with that one special person. But unfortunately, many of us spend much of our time on the bumper cars, ricocheting erratically from disappointing relationship to disappointing relationship.

We call this "dating."

Dating can be defined as a formally structured social ritual whereby single men and single women have dinner together to discover common interests and attitudes and to become better acquainted with the objective of finding a suitable companion who can:

Share with them a lifetime of spiritual communion or at least send them back to work on Monday morning covered with hickeys and claiming that they were savagely attacked by their vacuum cleaner.

Typically, people begin dating with high standards. They hold out for Mr. Right or Ms. Perfect. But with time and disappointment, they settle for Mr. Close Enough for Jazz or Ms. Reasonable Facsimile.

(This same pattern is seen elsewhere in nature. Fireflies flash their love lights—their Morse code of romance—seeking

a mate in the darkness. Early in the night they are picky, will respond only to the flash of certain other fireflies. By midnight, they are less picky, will settle for most any old firefly. By dawn they are desperate, will follow a turn signal home as long as it has a nice personality.)

THE WONDERFUL WORLD OF ONE

Mr. Right and Ms. Perfect, Mr. Close Enough for Jazz and Ms. Reasonable Facsimile, and those who date them usually are single. We all have been single at one time. Mother Teresa is single. The pope is single. God is single. Being single is a part of life. Like gas.

And today there are more singles than ever before. Young people are marrying later in life, the divorce rate is up, divorced people are slower to remarry, still other people are not marrying at all. Singles have become a legitimate subclass, a special interest group, like political parties, ethnic groups, religious denominations. Single people are devout members of the Little Church of the Divine Breath Mint.

He Said, She Said

Mr. Ross: "Oh, sure. But when was the last time Betsy mended my socks?"

Despite the large number of singles, society at large sometimes considers them to be incomplete, to lack a meaningful lifestyle. But being single can be wonderfully varied and satisfying. Oneness can be just as valid as twoness. And it takes up half the space. Single people are basically just like married people. If you prick them, do they not bleed? If you tickle them, do they not laugh? If you poison them, do they not die? If you cut them off in traffic, do they not go home and whine to their pets?

Indications That Your Date May Be a Loser

- Thinks the cutest characters in *The Wizard of Oz* are the winged monkeys.
- Asks if you'd like to double-date with his parole officer.
- Has the phone number of an exorcist on speed dial.
- Has charge account at Lawanda's House of Penicillin.
- On tax return she lists "hot pants" as a business expense.
- He served as technical adviser for the movie *Deliverance*.
- Has an imaginary friend named Skippy.

☛ You find yourself preferring to go out with Skippy.

☛ He claims that extraterrestrials have abducted him four times.

☛ Extraterrestrials find themselves preferring to abduct Skippy.

☛ Lists last book read as the Yellow Pages.

☛ At dinner, picks up a fork and asks, "What's this for?"

☛ Gives you an engagement ring purchased at a service station.

Single people fall into two categories: the so-far single and the suddenly single. The so-far single have not yet been married. The suddenly single have been married but have been rendered single through divorce or death or, on a really bad day, both. The main difference between the so-far single and the suddenly single is that the so-far single didn't have to order new checks.

Being single, like everything else in life, has advantages and disadvantages. The main advantage of being single is never having to consider anyone else. The main disadvantage of being single, likewise, is never having to consider anyone else.

Singles have more independence, fewer responsibilities, fewer obligations. But that also means that singles—no matter how active—spend a certain amount of time home all alone. Even Casanova had to go back to his house once in a while to rinse out his socks.

A single soon learns that being alone is not necessarily being lonely. When you are *alone* on a Friday night, you stay home and feed your goldfish; when you're *lonely* on a Friday night, you stay home and *dance* with your goldfish.

Being Single Is
....

☞ Hating to dine out alone. You feel stared at, gauche, as if the restaurant were a tuxedo and you were a pair of brown shoes.

☞ Being fixed up by well-meaning friends and relatives who know of someone who is a perfect match for you. Of course, these friends and relatives are the same people who, on aptitude tests, try to fit a round peg into a square hole, think that the seven of clubs and the four of diamonds are two of a kind, and wear brown shoes with a tuxedo.

☞ Falling asleep by counting the cracks in the plaster on the ceiling over your bed. How you wish that you had someone special there to help you count.

☞ Not knowing where your next argument is coming from.

☞ Trying to decide which tie to wear with nothing to do.

☞ Being awakened at 3 A.M. by a noise in your house and knowing that it has to be an intruder or your cat.

☞ Hoping it's an intruder so that you'll have someone different to talk to.

Ultimately, being single is like a slice of dry bread: It is what you make of it—crumbs or croutons. If you make crumbs of being single, at least there's no one there to nag you to clean up your mess. And if you make croutons of being single, the trick is to find the right person to provide the salad.

FIRST IS WORST

Unfortunately, science has failed to come up with a way for a single man and a single woman to begin dating without going on—gulp—their first date.

A first date is, like other firsts in life, a bittersweet milestone. Traditionally it has fallen to the man to ask out the woman. If a man wants to ask out a particular Ms. X, his is a simple two-step process:

1. Summon up more courage than he would need to go over Niagara Falls in a Big Mac wrapper.
2. Ask her.

If a woman wants to go out with a particular Mr. X, she has a choice:

1. Wait for him to ask her out.

   or

2. Ask him out.

Her first choice is passive. Waiting for him to ask her out means being patient and biding her time. But time is something she does not have a lot of. She feels herself bobsledding straight into orthopedic lingerie. Well, she can do some things to nudge her cause along. For example, if the two of them have never met, she can engineer an introduction—perhaps through a mutual acquaintance. Or she can engineer a coincidence. For example, if she knows that he shops at a certain supermarket, she can arrange to be there in the frozen food aisle when he is and to ram him "accidentally" from behind with her shopping cart and take it from there. Love among the fish sticks! Does ramming someone with a shopping cart sound too forced, too devious? You'd be surprised by how many times this ploy has sparked a romance. To say nothing of a lawsuit.

Her second choice—asking him out—is active. But even in today's liberated atmosphere, it is a very bold act for some women. Suddenly they know what it has been like for men for centuries. Suddenly the midheel pump is on the other foot. Many people of both genders exude negativity when they ask someone out for the first time. They approach the target of their amour, dig a toe in the ground, assume a sheepish look, and mumble, "Uh, I don't guess you'd want to go out with me, would you?"

This negativity is understandable. These people are dreading rejection. For many, fear of rejection ranks with the "Big Three" phobias: fear of flying, fear of spiders, and fear of public speaking. Add to those three the fear of rejection, and suddenly you're sitting in coach section and being turned down by an eight-legged Toastmaster.

But fear of rejection creates a self-fulfilling prophecy. Few people want to go out with someone who doesn't feel worthy. Those who date must be bold and take chances. Dating is not for the meek. Remember that although the meek shall inherit the Earth, they shall be too timid to show up at the reading of the will.

More Indications That Your Date May Be a Loser

- Considers Mussolini to have been a moderate.
- Receives Christmas cards from Ted Kaczynski.
- When he phones the suicide hot line, counselor's response is "Go for it!"
- Dial-a-Prayer refuses to accept her calls.
- Thinks "couch sores" should be a valid claim for disability income.
- Leaves a ring when he showers.
- Goodwill refuses to accept her discards.

☞ Uses Liquid Paper to fill in holes in his white socks.

☞ When asked to list weight, asks, "With or without eye shadow?"

☞ Lists favorite *Jeopardy* category as "Flatulence."

☞ Family history contains the phrase "So then, after my sister married my brother…"

☞ If he was shipwrecked and treading water in the Atlantic, dolphins would nudge him farther out to sea.

OK. The man or the woman has asked out the other and received an affirmative. The pressure is off, right? Hah! Not by a long shot.

After the man drives to the woman's home, approaches her door, and rings the bell, for man and woman alike the central nervous system goes to Code Red. "This is not a test. Woop woop woop!"

His underarms become moist enough to grow rice. Her heart begins to thump to the beat of Wagner's *Ride of the Valkyries*. This is because every first date is a crapshoot. What will she be like? What will he be like? Will they hit it off? In a matter of minutes the two of them could be suffering freezer burn just from dancing together. Or the two of them could be giving off more sparks than a Gremlin muffler dragging the ground.

Everything is magnified on a first date. Nothing is insignificant. First dates mean first impressions. A bad first impression means no second date. So everything conspires to ensure that every first date has at least one life-scarring moment of humiliation. It might be anything:

You drop a forkful of food between your plate and your mouth.

You have a thin string of saliva suspended between your upper and lower front teeth.

You say "imply" when you meant "infer."

"Omigod," you gasp when you realize your gaffe. "I am mortified. This is the worst moment of my life. Now this guy thinks I am a total feeb. I will die alone and childless and living in a cardboard shack with sixty-seven cats."

The brain, the Marquis de Sade of internal organs, never lets you forget such gaffes. Years later the brain will delight in torturing you by remembering them all, complete with sound effects and full color, just as it loves to remind you of all the other embarrassing, humiliating times in your life, dating back to the womb:

"Hey, remember that time when you were four and Jimmy Dale Squeedus saw your underpants?" your brain will ask gleefully.

"And remember that time when you were forty and making that big presentation at that board meeting and started coughing and couldn't stop and had to leave the room, and as you did, you tripped over your easel and fell down? And then, just when you were at your lowest, Jimmy Dale Squeedus walked in and saw your underpants?" Then the brain will giggle fiendishly and phone room service to order some more endorphins.

And if for some reason your brain *doesn't* remind you, your sixty-seven cats will.

THE DO'S AND DONATELLOS OF DATING

Singles have to put themselves into places and situations to meet other single people of the opposite sex. And the more opposite, the better. These places and situations include bars, malls, parties, and work- and church-related events. There singles face the pressure of having to be sensitive, suave, intelligent, witty, and interesting—all without flash cards. Here are some tips to help you:

Show intense interest in those you talk with. As they talk, look them in the eyes and bob your head thoughtfully, like one of those novelty dunking birds. If people are reticent, draw them out. Ask them lots of questions about their life story: "And after toilet training, then what?"

Be profound. Say things like, "I feel that the remarkable thing about Bach's music is the way it sounds."

Impress people by dropping names: "As I was saying to Galileo the other day..."

If that does not work, make a big production out of needing to use the phone. Then dial the number for time and temperature, jabber into the mouthpiece a minute, then hang up and come back to your cluster of fellow singles and explain, "Lee Iacocca had asked me to call and give him Mick Jagger's recipe for quiche lorraine."

If this does not impress, try a concentrated attack: "Oh, by the way, Madonna Baryshnikov Donatello Donna Mills Saul Bellow Jay Leno Brad Pitt Pitt the Elder Tom Brokaw Hirohito Lenny Bruce Bruce Springsteen Mrs. Wallis Simpson O. J. Simpson Homer Simpson Shadrach Meshach and Abednego Manny Moe and Jack and Jerry Mathers as the Beaver."

Keep live animals in your pants. To impress that special someone, pull out a mongoose and say, "Here. This is for you." She'll be so touched that she won't even notice that it isn't gift wrapped.

Dress to express your individuality. Bulky sweaters. Bold prints. Waxed paper. Wearing waxed paper makes a strong fashion statement. It says, "My Saran Wrap is still at the cleaners."

Act mysterious, as if you are hounded by a dark past or are the keeper of state secrets. Look distracted, worried, or pained. To achieve this, it helps if your waxed paper is riding up on you.

SO MANY MENUS, SO LITTLE TIME

Dating also creates the pressure of figuring out just what to do when two people go out. Couples have so many choices. Do they stay in or go out? If they stay in, do they rent a movie or watch TV? If they go out, do they go to a movie, and if so, which one of many multiplex theaters? Do they go to dinner, and if so, which cuisine? Chinese, Italian, French, Thai?

How much money do they spend? A couple of bucks to rent a video? Or a hundred bucks on a big night out? Even more if they end up needing a bail bondsman.

The mere act of agreeing on what to do on a date can be fraught with pitfalls. Typically, the man and woman strive to accommodate each other's wishes.

He: "How about a movie and dinner? Not that I care one way or another. Whatever *you* want to do."

She: "A movie and dinner are fine with me. I really have no preferences. Whatever *you* want to do."

Meanwhile, each is afraid that the other is just being polite while secretly thinking: "I'd rather walk barefoot through a snake pit than go to another movie and dinner."

So on their next date, they walk barefoot through a snake pit. He is bitten by a cobra; she elopes with the herpetologist.

ON THIS DATE IN HISTORY

These days, of course, dating is a well-established social institution. A confident, experienced man comes calling on the woman of his choice bearing the traditional gifts of dating—flowers and candy or, in the warmer climes, flowers and deodorant pads.

But dating has not always been the highly refined social ritual that fills men and women with pleasure, self-discovery, and, if done correctly, undiluted panic.

Nosiree. Dating as we know it is a relatively recent phenomenon. Dating, like the species, evolved slowly over the history of the human race. You don't think that humanity went from apes straight to John F. Kennedy, Jr., do you? No. In between were a million generations of Howard Stern.

In the beginning the Earth was void and without form. There was not much for couples to do on a date. The very first couples were simple one-celled organisms that had slithered up out of the primordial sea to stroll along the beach pseudopod in pseudopod. They had no fingers, no nose, and only the crudest idea of how to host a formal dinner party.

They also had no sexual organs. This was pretty dull but made for much less tension.

On a date they just moped around on the shore, waiting for singles bars to evolve.

By the time those one-celled organisms had evolved into primitive apelike cave dwellers, dating offered many more options. Couples could climb trees and pick fruit together. They could pick parasites off of each other. They could sit around the newly discovered phenomenon of fire and hold a stick over it and wait for someone to discover marshmallows.

Later, during the Dark Ages, most people were peasants who lived in abject squalor and ignorance, mired in superstition. A young man could never be sure that the young woman he went out with was not a witch. And if she *were* a witch, he had to be careful not to offend her. A general rule of thumb was that if, as the man kissed his date good night at her door, he was turned into a tree stump, he would probably *not* be asked inside for cappuccino.

For centuries, dating was not an option open to some young people. Their future mates had been predetermined for them in arranged marriages. Parents betrothed young children or even babies, who had no choice but to promise to love, honor, and patty-cake. It must have been sobering to these children to realize that in a few years, they would have to marry someone with whom all they currently had in common was diaper rash.

Mother Goose Update

Hey diddle diddle, the cat and the fiddle.

The cow jumped over the moon.

The little dog laughed to see such sport,

And the dish ran away with the spoon.

THE KITCHEN CABINET—Parents of an underage dish and a slightly tarnished spoon have filed missing-persons reports with police.

"Hey diddle diddle my hiney!" exclaimed the mother of the missing dish. "Those two kids have eloped together. I should have seen it coming. What kind of future do they have? What does a dish have in common with a spoon? Dinnerware and flatware are from two different worlds," she cried. "Kids at that age don't know what they want. Once she thought she was madly in love with a fork. Did that last? Hah! The first time he came home with a bent tine, she was outta there."

The father of the missing spoon agreed: "They're too young to settle down. We told him to date others. 'How about that nice lady cereal bowl who lives in the cupboard?' I asked him. 'She's eligible, nicely glazed, unchipped, and you'd always have lots of snap, crackle, and pop, if you know what I mean.' But did he listen?"

Police said there is no law against dinnerware and flatware marrying but added that such couples face a lifetime of prejudice and often are shunned by even the most liberal dishwashers.

As recently as one hundred years ago, dating was still primitive. Restaurants as we know them were rare. More likely, a couple would walk or travel by horse and buggy to a crude tavern for some tripe. One bowl, two straws. For entertainment, there were no movies. At most a couple might share a book, taking turns reading aloud to each other. Shy couples might just move their lips. Bolder couples might act out the action of the book. Reading *The Fall of the House of Usher* together was a leading cause of premature burial among dating couples.

Dating really came into its own in the twentieth century. And nothing revolutionized dating more than the automobile, which gave mobility and privacy to couples. Suddenly couples could get out of the house, away from their elders, and be alone up at Inspiration Point, where they could spend many romantic moments listening to each other's stomachs growl.

Aging: Life's Three—Or, We Hope, Four—Seasons

AGING IS inevitable. Everyone grows older, with the exceptions of Peter Pan, James Dean, and the Gerber Baby. Certainly seventy-six million baby boomers are growing older (note to self: buy more Polident stock). Aging is an integral part of life. Our age—or "season" of life—determines much about our goals, values, and outlooks and also influences how we relate to the opposite sex. Each season brings different expectations, privileges, and responsibilities. Indeed, the journey from diapers to Depends is long and complicated (to say nothing of damp).

PONTIACS, PIZZA, AND PUBERTY

The first season of life is youth. Young people have two primary goals:

1. Do as many reckless and potentially fatal things as possible and yet still somehow manage to stay alive to...

2. have sex every chance possible with other young people while wearing so many rings in pierced body parts that when they embrace, they suffer metal fatigue.

Teenagers become interested in the opposite sex at the onset of puberty.

Puberty is the hormonal Big Bang. After puberty, a 130-pound teenager is 25 pounds of jewelry, 25 pounds of trendy athletic shoes, and 80 pounds of hormones. Sometimes the hormones spill over into the athletic shoes, which is why so many teenagers slosh when they walk.

Approximately twenty-three minutes after entering puberty, a person falls in love for the first time. Suddenly she feels hot and cold, dizzy, clammy, weak, disoriented. Her pulse races, her heart pounds. If she were eight, it would be diagnosed as measles. But at fifteen, it's love. The major difference between measles and love is that she'll probably catch measles just once.

For teens, love and sex are the most adult things they do. After all, grown-ups are in love; adults have sex. Thus love and sex are entrees into adulthood, putting teens in heady company. Love and sex give teens something in common with parents, sports stars, movie stars, political leaders: "Hey, Bill, my chick goes wild when I blow in her ear. How about Hillary?"

Youth in love has no middle ground. Life is all highs or lows, either ecstasy or misery. On a graph, the emotional life of a teen would look like the EKG printout of an overweight person having a coronary. When two teens are attracted to each other, the smallest things in common are looked upon as eerie, magical, as proof of a love that was destined to be: "You're a carbon-based life-form?! *I'm* a carbon-based life-form! This is too weird!"

When boy and girl shyly hold hands for the first time, he marvels at the softness of her palm, the delicacy of her fingers. His heart soars. He dares to squeeze her hand, wondering if she will squeeze back. This is a big risk for him. His entire life is riding on this. If she returns his squeeze his ecstasy will multiply geometrically; he will rule the world. But if his squeeze should fall upon deaf fingers and go unanswered, he may grow despondent and bitter. He may never pop his knuckles again.

Ah, but the god of phalanges smiles upon him: She registers his squeeze and returns it. Without a word, he squeezes his reply. She squeezes back. It is a silent love song duet, sung in muscle contractions.

Even when boy and girl are separated, their romantic notions continue. Wherever he is, he pauses, looks up at the moon, and marvels to think that right at that moment, miles away, *she* could be gazing at the very same moon. And then the boy, with a tender sigh and a last look at *their* moon, goes back to vandalizing a cemetery.

SEE TOM CRUISE

(This section should be read while humming Chuck Berry's "No Particular Place to Go.")

The rituals of youth are many and strange. Many of these rituals involve cars. One of the most visible is cruising the main drag on Friday nights. In small towns and big cities, there is always one street that has everything that science has determined to be necessary to sustain teenage life: a mall or shopping

strip, gas station, video
store, music store, fast-
food joints, and, of
course, teens of
the opposite sex.

Along this
main drag, cars
filled with boys
and cars filled
with girls drive
back and forth end-
lessly, flirting, fighting,
seeing, and being seen,
swept up in the magic of motion and emotion. This is puberty on parade, a sort of hormonal ballet danced on radial tires.

Teens cruise the main drag in a long procession, hood to
trunk to hood, like those spiny lobsters that march single file
for miles across the ocean floor, head to tail to head. The difference is that lobsters seldom get into fistfights over who has
the coolest hubcaps.

For this procession, girls borrow the family cars or—better—drive their own cars. Boys, too, often drive their own
cars, which they bought and customized by working after
school and saving all their lunch money since the fifth grade.
A teen boy will invest every cent he has to ensure that his car
will make a statement to his peers. That statement is: "I have
twenty thousand dollars sunk in this car, and it takes every cent
I earn. But isn't it neat? Uh, are you going to eat all those
French fries?"

Teen boys keep their cars immaculate: washed, waxed, vacuumed. This is in sharp contrast to their bedrooms, which are

like the Okefenokee Swamp with wallpaper—dirt, dust, clutter, spilled Coke cans, half-eaten pizzas, and mounds of underwear that ferment until they evolve into primitive life-forms capable of walking, responding to stimuli, and, in some states, holding elected office.

Teen boys also keep their cars tuned and powerful. They spend all their money on souping up their cars until the cars are capable of 120 mph. Then, on Friday nights, they drive these cars up and down the main drag so slowly that in a race they could be outrun by a four-door kidney stone.

But cruising the main drag is not a quiet ritual. Typically the male cars have loud exhausts, rumbling like canned thunder, like God gargling. And both genders drive with their car radios cranked up to full volume, each rock song on the FM station relentlessly thumping its bass, as in *The Telltale Heart*, that story by Edgar Allan Poe about the guilt-ridden murderer who was tormented by the imagined sound of his dead victim's heartbeat until, finally, in desperation, he leaned over and switched to an all-news station.

With the invincibility that youth feel, not much scares teenagers. They will join street gangs, drive too fast, drive under the influence, experiment with drugs, batter their bodies with contact sports, and flirt with sexually transmitted disease without hesitation. What does scare teenagers is parents. Aaaaaaaeeeeeeeeee!

For a girl, one of life's scariest moments comes when her parents meet her date for the first time. Will they like him? Will they think she has good taste? Will there be a repeat of that unfortunate incident the last time she brought a boy home to meet her parents and her dad strip-searched him and confiscated several personal articles? The evening just wasn't the same without the switchblade.

Likewise, for a boy, one of life's scariest moments is meeting a date's parents for the first time. These are authority figures. They have the power of approval and disapproval. The father is imposing, intimidating. He is God with bifocals. After the father and the boy are introduced, the father takes the boy's fingerprints and mug shot. The mother runs a background check on the boy through the National Crime Information Center computer. While she is awaiting the printout, she sweetly offers him milk and cookies.

Thank goodness, with time this ritual gets slightly easier for a male. By the time he is forty and a date's parents are eighty, if they give him any lip, he can take away their walkers.

THOSE PESKY IN-BETWEEN YEARS

The second season of life is middle age. Middle-aged people are hard to figure. Young people are easy to figure—you know that they are thinking about sex. Old people are easy to figure—you know that they are thinking about how many more years before they are saluted by Willard Scott.

But the middle-aged are neither fish nor fowl, caught between youth and old age. It is an awkward age—too old for pimples, too young for probate. Everything about middle age is middle. We enjoy lower highs, but also suffer higher lows. Gone are the soaring ecstasies and the plunging depressions of youth. In Disney terms, youth is the roller coaster at Space Mountain; middle age is the boat ride through It's a Small World.

In middle age we may still be liberal and hip, still cool dudes and dudesses. We may still watch the Fox network and MTV and be able to listen to the latest music for upward of five minutes at a time. We may still believe that teenagers should be allowed to look any way they want. We may still believe that consenting adults should be able to do whatever they want behind closed doors as long as they tell us about it afterward.

But we also begin to exhibit the three sure signs of aging: gray hair, loss of muscle tone, and the tendency, while channel surfing, to pause longer and longer at the Rush Limbaugh show.

In middle age, love is more sensible, less hormone-driven than in youth. Not that middle age doesn't have its torrid moments. The middle-aged are sometimes astounded that they can feel a level of passion that rivals that of youth. Mother Nature has made sex such a powerful force that it persists past youth and into middle age. But in middle age it has to compete with other powerful forces such as career, family obligations, and crabgrass.

That's one reason that middle age is awkward: because a husband and a wife busily pursuing separate careers and raising a family are often too tired and too preoccupied at the end of the day to make love, although the more resourceful husbands and wives do exchange erotic stick-figure drawings on Post-it notes on the refrigerator door.

Subtle Changes in a Relationship over Time

	After two weeks	After ten years
Terms of endearment:	"Angel Drawers"	"Godzilla"
Bedtime:	7 P.M.	10 P.M.
Gifts:	Lingerie	Bunion pads
Last comment before falling asleep:	"You were incredible."	"If you snore again tonight, I'm leaving you."

First words upon waking:	"I've got three minutes before work. Wanna do it?"	"You snored all night. My lawyer will call your lawyer."
Preparation before bed:	Shower, condition hair, shave, trim and buff nails, brush teeth, floss, comb hair, pluck eyebrows, put on mood music, apply makeup, cologne, and whipped cream	Take milk of magnesia
Sleep in:	Skin	Ten-year-old flannel pajamas
Dinner topic:	How sexy the other looks	How cold this TV dinner is
Spend vacation:	On the same beach towel	Puttering around in garden and puttering around with new table saw
Vacation souvenir:	Terry-cloth burns on knees and elbows	Seventeen ant bites, three severed fingers

Middle age also is awkward because that is when many people find themselves divorced and suddenly dating again. Those who begin dating anew in middle age are understandably cautious, disillusioned. But they still want companionship, romance, and, yes, sex. They find themselves having to learn how to do it all over again. And no matter what anyone tells you, dating is *not* like riding a bicycle. You *do* forget how. Many a middle-aged person who begins dating again after years of monogamy has fallen off and skinned more than an elbow. For them, dating again brings insecurity and trepidation. The world has changed since they last dated. Customs have changed. *They* have changed. Life has worn down their confidence. Divorce has made them doubt their ability to sustain a relationship. For example, let's say that a woman of forty has spent years in a marriage and finds herself single again. It may be months before she has the interest or courage to date. All alone in her queen-size bed at night, she feels anything but royal. She tries not to wonder what her ex-husband is doing right at that moment. But, of course, her brain, being the cruel and spiteful organ that it is, comforts her by imagining him being shown around Vegas on the lean, tanned arms of two six-foot-tall chorus girls.

"It figures," the ex-wife thinks bitterly as she drifts off into a fitful sleep. "When he was married to me, he had a *fear* of heights!"

When she is at last ready, our divorced woman of forty may find herself dressing right beside her teenage daughter on a Friday night—both of them preparing to go out on dates. As the mother slips into what she perceives to be her best drop-dead outfit, her daughter, who is always quick to lend filial empathy and support, assesses Mom's killer look and says: "Gawd, Mom. You're not going to go out looking like *that*, are you? What a geek!"

If mother and daughter should happen to cross paths later that night while each is out on the town, the mother, with the profound love that only a parent can know, will key the brat's car.

But dating in middle age after a divorce can also be exciting and rejuvenating. Our divorced woman finds, to her surprise and relief, that she is still attractive to the opposite sex, that there are millions of men out there who, unlike her ex-husband, have never seen her sick, never seen her moody, never seen her the first thing in the morning after the office Christmas party.

But middle-aged couples who are dating find themselves set in their ways, rigid and inflexible. Old habits and outlooks are hard to break. Whereas when she was twenty years younger, our divorced woman might have overlooked her beau's consistently leaving the lid off the mustard jar, now she evaluates him with a mental list of pros and cons:

Pros	Cons
Intelligent	Leaves lid off mustard jar
Affectionate	
Charming	
Clean	
Sensitive	
Witty	
Attractive	
Stable	
Lots in common	
Likes my kids	
My kids like him	

She looks at the list and says, "Hmmm. Too close to call."

Middle-aged dating couples also often have children living at home. Their feelings must be considered, their needs met. This means that for the man and woman, passion sometimes must take a backseat to carpooling eighth-graders. And, of course, marriage among the middle-aged often creates blended families. Shortly after the last kernel of rice has bounced off the bride and groom, they realize that their two broods are *not* going to be the Brady Bunch.

If *The Brady Bunch* show were updated for the '90s, mother Carol would now have her own successful career, Gold Card, and therapist; father Mike would be spending sixty hours a week at his architecture office and coming home only long enough to have chest pains. Maid Alice would be stealing from the Bradys to support her Chippendales habit. Daughter Marcia would be bisexual and playing lead guitar in a punk rock band called Vermin Entrails; daughters Jan and Cindy would be exchanging E-mail with a psychopath on the Internet; and sons Peter, Greg, and Bobby would be on Ritalin and hoping to grow up to become either priests or hit men, whichever get to meet more chicks.

But despite the challenges of middle age, there definitely are rewards. By middle age we have lost the insecurities and impetuosities of youth. We know ourselves better, have fewer illusions. We have wisdom, experience, stability. In fact, there is a period in middle age when we wouldn't change places with a person twenty years younger. This period lasts until we get dizzy bending over to apply a bunion pad.

Middle-aged people are at the pinnacle of their success. They have mastered the three keys to career success: experience, knowledge, and the ability to write vaguely menacing memos.

But there is a tradeoff for success. Because middle-aged couples have more, they also have more to argue about—money, career, children, how their time is spent. Successful middle-aged men and women worry more, work harder and longer, and harbor 95 percent of the world's known reserves of stomach acid. The life experiences and attitudes that brought them success also keep them from being able to relax and enjoy that success. Even the Bible addressed this irony: "What is a man profited if he shall gain the whole world but forget how to boogie?"

He Said, She Said

Mr. Anthony: "Yeah, Susan has her face on a dollar. But does she ever have change for a pay toilet?"

READY, SET, SQUAT

Middle age is a time of transition. In middle age, there comes a day, a watershed moment, when we trade in the sports car for a sensible sedan or a minivan. The man trades his briefs for boxer shorts, his tight jeans for slacks so roomy in the seat that he has room for a second butt, should he ever desire to add on. The woman trades her short leather skirt for a tailored business suit. She retires her push-up bra and trades her bikini panties for underwear that, in a midair emergency, could double as a parachute.

In middle age, our bodies also change. We tire more easily. When we go out to paint the town, we can no longer finish even the primer coat.

Our eyesight begins to change. Distant objects are sharp enough, but close objects become a bit fuzzy. It must be the same way that robbers see things when they wear pantyhose pulled over their head. In other words, a middle-aged person can't see well enough to hold up a liquor store, but can see well enough to drive the getaway car.

Seventy-six million baby boomers are going through this change in eyesight. You may have noticed them at the office, squinting their way into the mailroom instead of the rest room by mistake. No wonder the mail clerk looks so bitter.

Mother Goose Update

**Three blind mice. Three blind mice. See how they
run. See how they run.
They all ran after the farmer's wife,
Who cut off their tails with a carving knife.
Did you ever see such a sight in your life
As three blind mice?**

FARMINGTON—Onetime farmer's wife Margery Daw, who
gained notoriety two years ago when she was convicted
on three counts of violating Criminal Code 123.77
(assault on a visually challenged rodent) after unsuccess-
fully claiming PMS as a defense, was released from prison
today.

At her well-publicized trial, where she was defended by
Water Rat from "The Wind in the Willows," Ms. Daw had
claimed: "I had been having a real bad day. My head was
pounding. I was bloated. The least little thing irritated
me. Then these three mice appeared from nowhere and
began to run after me. They were tapping those little
white canes. And they had those bristly little whiskers
and twitching noses and those gross tails. Yeech! I just
snapped."

Ms. Daw, who divorced her farmer husband while in
prison, said she plans to marry her former defense
attorney.

"Margery is totally rehabilitated," said Mr. Rat, "and I
am sure that we'll live happily ever after. Although I do
plan to sleep with one eye open."

We also begin to put on weight. Our center of gravity, once located above our waist, begins to slip southward, ever southward. Eventually our navel is somewhere in Peru. The Incas, like the mail clerk, are not pleased.

So, to remain attractive to the opposite sex, we begin to exercise. We jog, we go to health clubs, we do calisthenics. Humans are the only animals that exercise, laugh, cry, or blush. Sometimes all in the same squat-thrust.

We get involved in sports such as cycling, tennis, handball, and baseball. With middle-aged logic, we feel that being killed at age sixty-one by heart disease is tragic, but that being killed at age forty-one by a line drive is noble.

But then all too often we become discouraged, give up our good intentions, and go back to our sedentary lifestyles. This usually happens when we realize that we have to walk briskly for an hour to burn off the calories contained in a single slice of apple pie. This cruel inequity between the calories contained in the foods we love and the calories burned in the exercise we hate is, to the middle-aged, proof that 1. there is no God; and 2. He doesn't have to watch His weight.

TIC, TACKY, TUCK

There is another challenge lurking out there for the middle-aged. Just when it seems that we have it all—financial security, a home, a career, a loving family, common sense, good health—we throw it all away and go slightly insane. Yes, the midlife crisis. Aaaaaaaeeeeeeeeeeeee!

The midlife crisis usually begins when we are doing something monotonous—mowing the lawn, making lunch for the kids. We begin to question everything we have done in our life so far—career choice, house, spouse, family. We feel trapped in the American dream. Our nice home in the suburbs suddenly seems like a prison, our station wagon like a hearse.

We realize that life is half over and feel that not only is life passing us by, but also that it slows down only long enough to moon us.

We desperately want to regain our youth, to be cool again, conveniently forgetting that we never were cool in the first place.

We feel that we haven't accomplished much and chastise ourselves with unflattering comparisons. After all, we remind ourselves, by age forty Edison had already invented the phonograph. By age forty Bell had already invented the telephone, using it to call up Edison to ask him to please turn down his phonograph. By age forty Beethoven had already composed his first five symphonies and had begun to go deaf, eventually calling Edison to ask him to turn his phonograph back up.

Sometime around forty we realize our limits. Limits are a pretty hard truth to bump into during the long dark night of middle age. Especially if we are barefoot at the time. In middle age we realize that we are as smart, as talented, as successful, and as attractive as we will ever be. Napoleon was forty-six when he realized that he was probably as tall as he was ever going to be. He reacted to this hard truth as any rational megalomaniac would: He had France raised eight inches.

In midlife, a man realizes that his idea of being independent is to order salad when everyone else at the table orders soup. His idea of taking risks is to leave the house without an umbrella. He needs two days' notice to be spontaneous.

He sees himself becoming surrounded by the icons of advancing age—bifocals, denture adhesives, and boxer shorts—and feels them mocking him. Only you who have been mocked by boxer shorts have known true despair.

He becomes convinced that only a sports car or, better, a motorcycle will save him. He wants to hit the open road, follow the sun, and find himself. He wants to have adventures. He knows that deep inside him an outlaw is yearning to break free: "Yes, sir. I am Johnny Gypsy. Adventure is my mistress. Excitement is my muse. Danger is my cleaning lady (she comes in twice a week to scare the dust)."

Likewise, a woman fears growing old. She does some calculating one day about forty and realizes that she has stretch marks older than Pamela Anderson Lee.

For a woman, age comes creeping on little crow's feet. She fears finding herself on the Grim Reaper's "A" list and realizing that she didn't really *live* life.

She fears that she is in a rut. *Rut* is a dandy verb, but it's a nowhere noun.

A midlife crisis causes some to feel the need to reaffirm their sexuality, their attractiveness to the opposite sex, preferably with a total stranger, someone who has not seen them every morning for the last twenty years without makeup and unshaven and grumpy, someone who has never watched them pumice their feet or trim their nose hairs, someone who was not there when they went through childbirth or a hernia operation or their disco phase.

A man develops an intense interest in young women with huge man-made, cantilevered breasts. He asks his wife if they can adopt a Dallas Cowboys cheerleader.

A woman finds herself attracted to outlaw types, to tattooed men, to younger men. She finds herself mentally undressing a well-built sack boy. She flirts, winking at him shamelessly. He thinks that the poor old woman has a nervous tic.

Obviously, this is a very trying time for the partners of such men and women. The partners feel rejected, confused, helpless. What can they do? Should a wife try keeping her temporarily insane husband in the marriage by keeping up— by dressing twenty years too young and acting like a hot young thing? Not unless she feels that she isn't getting enough ridicule in her diet.

Should a husband dye his graying hair, get a tummy tuck, and become some Robin Hood–type outlaw to retain his wife's interest? No. That would be socially irresponsible, and he doesn't have the knees for tights.

Fortunately, the midlife crisis doesn't last. Usually we come to our senses, realizing how much we have and how much we treasure our lifestyle and the people in it.

A man sells the motorcycle after he realizes that the human body is an incredibly fragile thing of beauty that loses much of that beauty when spread-eagled across the grille of an oncoming Coupe de Ville.

A woman mothballs the miniskirt and the halter top when she realizes that those sack boys she is flirting with may be young and virile, but that communication with them breaks down rapidly after "You want paper or plastic?"

And when we come back from our detour into insanity, we hope that our mates are there waiting faithfully to take us back and, with truly humbling love and understanding, to remind us every day for the rest of our lives how stupid we acted.

OUT TO PASTURE? BULL!

The third season of life is old age. Inevitable though aging is, when we are young the prospect of old age is like crime or catastrophic disease or having chef Paul Prudhomme fall on us. We think: "It can't happen to *me*." When we are young, being old is something that happens to other people, usually Republicans.

Predictably, as we age, we constantly redefine the concept of "old." When we are ten, old is twenty. When we are twenty, old is forty. By the time we are eighty, old is people with the words *the late* in front of their name.

This third season of life has changed a lot in recent years. No longer are old people worn-out, bitter, desiccated, feeble grumps. Today people live longer and remain physically active and mentally alert longer. They continue to work, to play sports, and, yes, to have sex at an age that their middle-aged children find vaguely disgusting.

Older people are survivors. They have beaten the odds just to reach this season of life—they have avoided death by disease, by war, by random big city violence and freak bowling accident.

And if they are married to their original spouses from youth, they have, again, beaten the odds. Forty or fifty years of marriage to one person is a miracle in this age of disposable relationships. For most people, it takes three spouses to rack up that many years of marriage. Two people married that long have seen much, felt much, won and lost much together. They have somehow remained understanding and flexible enough to stay together despite family meddling, outside temptations, midlife crises, and changes brought on by time. She has survived his sports car, country western, and leisure suit phases; he has survived her phases as a brunette atheist, a redheaded vegetarian, and a communist with blonde highlights.

People may stay vital longer than ever, but aging does bring some inevitable changes. There are mental changes. Something in the DNA of women after sixty makes them put out feeders for birds and squirrels. Something in the DNA of men after sixty makes them begin to wear jumpsuits.

If we spend the first third of life wishing we were older and the second third wishing we were younger, we spend the final third wishing we could remember where we left our reading glasses.

Our priorities also change as we age. We become more pragmatic. When a man is twenty and sees an attractive woman across a crowded room, he wonders what kind of underwear she is wearing. When he is sixty, he wonders if she has adequate life insurance.

A woman of twenty shouts, "Let's change the world!" A woman of sixty shouts: "Let's change the cat's litter box. It's closer."

And then there are physical changes. As a youth, you think of your body as a wondrous machine, a willing and tireless servant that takes you to some great parties. As you get older, you think of your body more as a convenient place to keep your surgery scars.

Body and mind begin to get into shouting matches with each other. The body shouts to the mind: "You're always thinking about World War II when you need to be thinking about driving this car."

The mind replies to the body: "Oh, yeah? Well, you just keep your hands on the wheel and your eyes on the road. You almost ran over General Patton!"

But despite such changes, these are the golden years. And they are doubly golden when shared. Older people have watched their children move away or develop busy lives of their own. They have watched their friends and colleagues begin to show up in the obituary column. So they cherish a mate more than ever. A mate plays many roles in the third season of life: partner, companion, defender, beneficiary. No one wants to grow old alone. There'd be no one there to help if we fall and break a hip, no one there to share the beautiful singing of a robin with, no one there to listen to us complain that that darned robin's singing is keeping us from taking our nap.

In the third season of life, many an older woman finds herself single because she has outlived her husband. Many an older man finds himself single because his wife couldn't *stand* those jumpsuits. But none of them is ready to stop living and loving. Older single men and women who meet have fewer illusions, are more pragmatic in what they are looking for in a mate: "Can you open a child-proof medicine bottle? Are your teeth paid for? How many of your organs are original equipment?"

Whether married or dating, older people have much to enjoy. They are retired, the house is paid off, the children are grown and gone. At last a man and a woman have the time to do whatever they want. Many of them travel. They take Caribbean cruises and packaged tours of Europe, tramping tirelessly through cathedrals and museums and historic birthplaces. They set off to see America on their own, manhandling a huge fuel-guzzling Winnebago (Indian for "Fill 'er up") motor home that comes with TV, microwave, and its own OPEC country.

They have the time to spend with their grandchildren and to undo ten years of responsible parenting in a single spoiled weekend.

They have the time to write reactionary letters to the editor.

They have the time to share a hobby such as gardening and to get into long, pointless arguments over which one of them left the pruning shears out in the rain.

A woman has the time to devote to genealogy, spending many happy hours tracing her ancestors all the way back to 1620, when a family member known as Edward the Irritating sailed to America on the *Mayflower* but was so obnoxious that halfway over the other Pilgrims bound and gagged him and threw him into the hold, where he stayed until 1693, when someone finally remembered that he was there and at last came to make sure that he was still tied up.

A man has the time to sit on the porch and spit and whittle and think about things: "My Social Security check is late again. This laxative isn't working. God, Robin Leach's voice makes me cringe. That old woman is crazy—I'm not the one who left those darned shears out in the rain. I'm the one who left the grandkids out in the rain."

Yes, youth, middle age, and old age can be fulfilling seasons for men and women. And afterward, let us hope that there is a fourth season for us to share. Ideally, two people will grow old together and stay together right up to the end of a long and fulfilling life. Because when we begin the inevitable journey to what Shakespeare called "that undiscovered country from whose bourn no traveler returns," it sure would be nice to take a date.

And the Winnebago.

CHAPTER Eight

Communication:
Well, Shut My Mouth!

WE HUMANS are the only species with a highly developed power of speech and a complex and richly textured vocabulary that allow us, when we are introduced to someone—no matter how important and intimidating that personage—to say:

"Meet to glad you."

If we have such a highly developed power of speech, why do we have so much trouble communicating, especially between genders? Many of the problems between men and women center around communication.

Ironically, women and men share communication traits of the pets that traditionally are associated with their opposite gender. Women are thought of as cat lovers, men as dog lovers. But in their communication style, women are more like dogs, men are more like cats.

Dogs are guileless, extroverted, an open book. You always know what a dog is thinking. Dogs bark, they jump, they slobber. A dog wears its feelings on its sleeve. For example, when Spot wags his tail, he is happy. When Spot slinks, he is contrite or afraid. When Spot attaches himself to your minister's leg, he is missing the Dalmatian that used to live next door.

Cats are inscrutable, independent, secretive. For example, when a cat swishes its tail, you seldom know what it is thinking.

The cat might be saying, "I am excited." The cat might be saying, "I am miffed." The cat might be saying, "A minister's leg, Spot? I didn't know you were so religious."

Likewise, women are more open and talkative than men. They share their feelings. They are, for the most part, direct. For example, when a woman says to a man, "I am very angry at you for the way you behaved at Bill and Edna's party last night," he can be pretty sure of two things:

1. She is very angry at him for the way he behaved at Bill and Edna's party last night.

2. The next time he is found in a closet performing the Heimlich maneuver on Edna, she had jolly well better be choking on something

He Said, She Said

Mr. Arc: "Sure, Joan heard the voices of saints. But did she hear me say that I smelled something burning?"

Men, like cats, keep their feelings to themselves. This drives women crazy. When a man does not talk about his feelings, his silence is too open to interpretation and misinterpretation. Sometimes a woman interprets a man's silence according to her own outlook on life: If she is an optimist, and he is silent, he is not complaining, so he must be happy, content. No news is good news. If she is a pessimist, and he is silent, she imagines the worst: "Omigod! What is he not telling me? He's dying. He's been fired, and we're broke! He doesn't find me attractive anymore!"

By the time she finds out that he just didn't have much to say that day, she has bought a tombstone, held up a liquor store, and undergone liposuction and a makeover.

TO UNGH OR NOT TO UNGH

Men have always been this way. William Shakespeare, who so eloquently expressed the entire range of human emotions on paper in his plays and sonnets, would sit around the cottage and have very little to say to Anne Hathaway. He'd just grunt whenever she would try to draw him out:

"A penny for your thoughts, Bill."

"Ungh."

"Is work on your new play going well?"

"Ungh."

"Boy, how 'bout that Renaissance, eh?"

"Ungh."

This is what started those theories that Shakespeare did not really write the works that are attributed to him. Anne Hathaway just couldn't believe that a man so inarticulate with his mouth could be so articulate with his pen. She began to suspect that someone else—probably Francis Bacon—must have written all those plays and sonnets. Meanwhile, Mrs. Bacon was trying to pry a few syllables out of her Francis:

"So, do you think this Protestant thing will catch on?"

"Ungh."

Sometimes when a woman is trying to get a man to open up and talk to her, she feels as if the two of them are playing a game of charades. She has to coax each word out of him:

"OK. Is it a song title?"

"Ungh."

"It is. Ok. How many syllables?"

"Ungh."

"Five. OK. First word?"

"Ungh."

"OK. Rhymes with 'Stiff.' Riff? Cliff? If?"

"Ungh."

"Bingo. If. Second word?"

"Ungh."

"OK. Sounds like 'eye.' Spy? Cry? I?"

"Ungh."

"Bingo! I. OK, song title of six syllables that starts with 'If I.' Hmmm. Is it 'If I Had a Hammer?'"

"Ungh."

"Bingo! Awww. Have the neighbor kids been stealing your tools again?"

"Ungh."

ACTIONS FIX LOUDER THAN WORDS

Whereas women talk, men act. Men are oriented toward results and achievement, toward solving problems and fixing things. In a way, men talk with their hands. It's certainly not as articulate, but when men can't or won't express their feelings with words, they sometimes express their feelings by fixing things. Fixing a woman's things is one of the highest forms of affection that a man can bestow on her.

So maybe women should try looking at it this way:

If he fixes your living room lamp, think of it as the equivalent of his giving you a big hug.

If he installs a 220-volt outlet in your laundry room, think of it as the equivalent of his saying, "I love you."

If he rewires your entire house, think of it as the equivalent of his saying, "My life would be a dark and starless sky, a meaningless void stretching into infinity, without the sunshine of your love to illuminate my soul and brighten my every moment."

There. Doesn't looking at it that way make you women feel better?

We thought not.

Mother Goose Update

There was an old woman who lived in a shoe. She had so many children she didn't know what to do.

SOLE CITY—A local woman known for her fertility and unusual domicile is celebrating the sounds of silence these days.

"Yes, the last child has grown up and left home," said the old woman who lived in a shoe. "To this day I don't know exactly how many kids we had over the years. It was either twelve or thirty-nine. My OB-GYN explained to me that I am as fertile as an Iowa cornfield. My husband could just touch me and I'd puff up like a pan of Jiffy Pop. Of course, he could leave home every day and go off to work. Me, I had to stay here in this shoe, knee-deep in babies and foot powder. I love every cotton-pickin' one of my younguns, but sometimes it just overwhelmed me.

"We outgrew this shoe in no time. I'd tell my husband, 'This penny loafer is just too small for us. We need at least a wing tip or a cowboy boot.' But just try to find a furnished cowboy boot that's located in a good neighborhood and hasn't been tackied up with beer cans and Patsy Cline posters.

"So we toughed it out. And we survived somehow. All the kids are grown and gone now. The shoe is empty. Finally. It's just the two of us here. In fact, the mister and me will be celebrating our twentieth anniversary next month."

Asked what she plans to give her husband for that special occasion, she said: "First I was going to give him a new golf bag. Then I was going to give him a set of socket wrenches."

So which did she settle on, she was asked.

"I'm going to give him a vasectomy."

Sometimes, women, too, say very little about their feelings. A wife may come home from work in a terrible mood: She slams doors, breaks dishes. She cries. She throws herself into preparing dinner, rattling pots and pans, using a large machete to chop the salad.

The husband asks, "Is anything wrong, Dear?"

"Nothing."

A woman's "Nothing" is not the same as a man's "Ungh." Her "Nothing" does not mean that she has nothing on her mind, and it is not to be taken literally. She does want to talk, but she may not be quite ready yet or she may want the man to draw her out, to show his concern so that she can vent her feelings. Most experts agree that if the man elects to draw her out, he should wait until she has finished chopping the salad.

In general, women are more in touch with their feelings. They get problems off their chests by talking about them. They don't hold things in. Talking for them is cathartic. For a man, it takes more to nudge him over the talk threshold. His chatostat is set higher. For example, when a relationship begins to sour, whereas the woman will begin talking about it—expressing her feelings, asking his—at, if not before, the first hint of potential disharmony, the man will not begin talking about the relationship until the wife has actually run away with the Domino's pizza deliveryman and has left behind a note saying she's sorry and there's a large double-cheese mushroom-and-olive in the oven.

Men hold problems in. A man is like an oyster. A minor problem is a grain of sand that gets into his shell and irritates him. Rather than talk about it, get it out into the open, deal with it, and get over it, he coats it with layer after layer of repression and denial until eventually he has a pearl of pain about the size of a beach ball inside him. Those big bellies you see on men—those aren't beer bellies; they're pearls of pain.

Then one day, without warning the oyster buys a rifle, a scope, and several hundred rounds of ammunition and climbs to the top of a tower, and the next thing we know, his wife is on the evening news as Ted Koppell asks her if she had suspected that something was bothering her late husband.

"Did he say anything to you to indicate he was unstable?"

"Yes, he did say one thing, although I didn't pay any attention to it at the time."

"And what was that?"

"'Ungh.'"

... AND NOTHING BUT THE TRUTH—HONESTLY

The powerful communication skills that men and women have also enable them to lie, exaggerate, mislead, embellish, and otherwise take liberties with the truth.

Lies That Men Tell Women

- ☞ "I promise that all we'll do is cuddle."
- ☞ "That bra was in the glove compartment when I bought the car."
- ☞ "Cleavage? No, I didn't notice that woman's cleavage."
- ☞ "I *am* listening. I heard every word you said."
- ☞ "Mmmm-mmm. Your pickled peaches. My favorite!"
- ☞ "No, you don't snore."
- ☞ "You wear those thirty extra pounds really well."
- ☞ "That wasn't me. It was the dog."

Lies That Women Tell Men

- ☞ "Those love handles look cute on you."
- ☞ "Our book club meeting lasted until 2 A.M."
- ☞ "Sure, I'd *love* to go to the rattlesnake roundup with you."

- ☞ "Nothing's wrong. I *always* cry during 'Roadrunner' cartoons."
- ☞ "You are definitely the best lover I've ever had."
- ☞ "Honey, you're not small. You're compact."
- ☞ "Don't feel bad, Honey. Twenty-four seconds can be plenty with the right man."
- ☞ "Of course I did. If I could fake anything that well, I'd be cranking out Picassos and forging Voltaire's signature on my grocery lists."

LITTLE WHITE LIE SEEKS SOUL MATE

A perfect example of exaggeration by men and women is singles ads. You may have read them, answered them, even placed them yourself. Such ads create the impression that your hometown is bursting at the city limits with the most sincere, attractive, charming, sophisticated, intelligent, sensitive, and disease-free single folks imaginable. Soon some of them will have to be bused to Wyoming to alleviate the crowding.

Singles typically compose such ads during long, lonely weekend nights as they sigh heavily and listen to the phone not

ring. As they compose their ads they, shall we say, give themselves the benefit of the doubt. Thus "bright" is used to describe a woman who routinely gets lost on her way to work. "Handsome" is used to describe a man who is often mistaken for a philodendron. By other philodendrons.

It's always been this way. Here's an early singles ad that appeared in a London newspaper in the 1500s:

> **Single white male king, 40ish, is tired of relationships that don't last. I am pleasingly plump and jolly, but, alas, a widower. Would you enjoy cozy nights around my castle with fine food and wine, watching the executioner sharpen his ax? Would you enjoy wearing priceless gold necklaces around your pretty little neck? Then let's take a whack at it. Reply with a wallet-sized oil portrait of yourself to Henry, P.O. Box VIII.**

Here's how to read between the lines of today's singles ads:

> **Libra male with the soul of a poet seeks that special lady. Let's share quiet times in my world, full of flowers, soft music, satin, and mahogany.**

The soul of a poet: His ex-wives are named Mindy, Cindy, Lindy, and Wendy.

Quiet times in my world, full of flowers, soft music, satin, and mahogany: This man is an undertaker.

> **Sports-oriented woman seeks mate. Cultured. Neat and clean. Very giving.**

Sports-oriented: Owns her own tennis racket, knows which end of it you putt with.

Cultured: Most of her dates come from a petri dish.

Neat: She is anal-retentive.

Clean: During the night of a full moon she must be hosed down.

Very giving: She has seven of the Top Ten social diseases.

> **Single man active in hematology. Nonmaterialistic and outdoorsy. Good with my hands. Laid-back.**

Active in hematology: He gets most of his income by selling his blood.

Nonmaterialistic: He lives in a packing crate.

Outdoorsy: The crate is located in a vacant lot.

Good with my hands: He built the crate himself.

Laid-back: Takes his teeth out at parties.

> **Outgoing woman, sturdy but active, seeks mate. Willing to raise your children and mime. Interests include music, literature, Druidism.**

Sturdy: Her thighs are often mistaken for grain silos.

Willing to raise your children and mime: This could be a misprint of "Willing to raise your children and *mine*," or perhaps deep down this woman is looking for Marcel Marceau.

Druidism: This cult worshiped trees; this woman believes that a 2x4 died for our sins.

> **Fun-loving, financially secure man seeks a woman to take long, romantic walks with. Well-read, never far from a book.**

Fun-loving: He has a dribble glass.

Financially secure: The dribble glass is paid for.

Take long, romantic walks: He doesn't own a car.

Never far from a book: Being four foot eleven, he often stands on an unabridged dictionary.

> **Professional woman, 34, is tired of the bar scene. Active in oil and gas, stocks and bonds.**

Tired of the bar scene: People keep stepping on her hands.

Active in oil and gas: This woman is a fry cook.

Stocks and bonds: She is also a sadist.

> **Successful male executive, equally at ease on the town
> or on safari. Knows a pas de deux from a do-si-do. 42,
> 188, 5-10.**

Equally at ease on the town or on safari: He wears a silk loincloth.
42, 188, 5-10: These are his age, weight, and height, right?
Wrong. They indicate his IQ, weekly wage, and how many
years in prison he served after his *last* date.

IMPROVE YOUR RESPONSE ABILITY

One of the biggest problems in communication is not knowing how the other gender will respond to what we say. Here
are two charts to help:

When a Woman Says...	*A Man Thinks...*
"Drop dead, jerk. I wouldn't go out with you if I was a carrot stick and you were the last dip on Earth!"	"All *right*! This chick is starting to dig me."
"I'd be delighted to go out with you, but I don't want to get serious about anyone right now."	"I wonder what we should name our first child."
"Would you like to come in for a quick nightcap?"	"Oh, man! I'm glad I brought my toothbrush and pajamas!"
"That man you saw me with is just a friend."	"I wonder how long she's been sleeping with him."

"Yes, as a matter of fact I *would* mind going to the tractor pull tonight."

"Okay, she wants to see just the first few contests."

"I think it's time we made a real commitment to this relationship."

"Hmmm. I wonder when the next Greyhound leaves town."

When a Man Says...   A Woman Thinks...

"Okay, so maybe I've had a beer or two."

"Yeah, he and the Astrodome are the Coors company's biggest accounts."

"You look fine."

"Omigod! He thinks I look like a frumpy ol' fishwife!"

"You look hot, hot, hot."

"Omigod! He thinks I look merely adequate!"

"You look like the most irresistible goddess who ever descended from Olympia."

"Okay. Maybe I do look good. I'll just add a little more eyeliner."

"I believe in equal rights for women."

"He wants to go Dutch treat."

"I'll call you soon."

"He'll call me soon."

WHAT YOU HEARD IS NOT WHAT I SAID

Another problem that the two genders have in communicating is not knowing what the other means. So here are two charts to help:

When a Woman Says...	*She Means...*
"Sorry. I'm busy this weekend, but give me a call another time."	"The next time you phone me, Buster, I'll have caller ID."
"Yeah, okay. I guess I'll go out with you."	"Why not? It beats scrubbing the mildew in my shower stall."
"No, really, my parents like you just fine."	"They are enrolling me in a convent this weekend."
"Does this dress make me look fat?"	"I am feeling insecure. Please reassure me that I am still attractive. A lie would be acceptable, but a sincere low moan would be ideal."
"Maybe you shouldn't yodel so loudly, Dear. This is a *Japanese* restaurant."	"Why don't we just set the saki on my side of the table for a while."
"Why don't you let me pick out a suit for you, Honey?"	"What you're wearing looks like an explosion at a clown college."

"You look tired, Sweet. I'd be glad to drive."

"Let's see if we can go just one trip without you mooning a highway patrolman."

When a Man Says...	He Means...
"Hi. What's your name?"	"I wish to have intercourse with you."
"Hi. Is this the classroom where Geometry 101 meets?"	"I wish to have intercourse with you."
"Hi. You have a lovely smile."	"I wish to have intercourse with you."
"Do you want paper or plastic?"	"I wish to have intercourse with you."
"Arrrrrgghh-h-h-h-h-h! Please help me. I am trapped under this overturned thrashing machine, and many important bones have been crushed!"	"Call the paramedics. Later, meet me in Intensive Care. I wish to have intercourse with you."

Nine

Trouble:
Love's Labor's Lester

IF MEN AND WOMEN are so attracted to each other, if pairing is the goal of so many billions of people throughout human history, why is it so difficult for men and women to find the right mate? Why is it so difficult for them to stay with that mate? Why can't a husband and a wife discuss money without getting into such an argument that their banker has to come in and shoot one of them with a tranquilizer dart?

At first glance, the mere math of romance would seem so favorable for each of us to find the right mate. After all, there are 5 billion people in the world. There must be thousands of perfect matches for each person, right? But let's look at this math more closely. Let's say that you are a single woman. And because you don't have a valid passport, we will confine your search for your perfect match to America. Still, that's 250 million people. Wow! Ah, but right away you rule out half the population as being of the wrong gender. But that means you still have 125 million men to choose from. So many men, so little estrogen.

But of those 125 million, you rule out 50 million as married, 30 million as too young, 20 million as too old. Then you rule out 8 million men who are not attracted to women. These reduce your man pool to 20 million.

"So what?" you say. "For God's sake, I'm looking for just one man, not the cast of *Bonanza*."

Ah, but of those remaining
20 million men:

6,669,455	are in prison.
1	is O. J. Simpson.
5,601,627	drink too much.
3,492,112	can't commit.
1,198,332	are married to their jobs.
871,002	think a woman's place is in the kitchen.
766,543	think a woman's place is at the nudie bar.
681,402	are carrying a torch for their ex-wives.
679,243	have irreconcilable religious or political differences with you.
20,102	think they are God's gift to women.
20,101	think they are God's gift to gambling.

78	move their lips when they read a stop sign.
1	is that shoe salesman who told you that the only way you'll ever fit into a size eight again is by: 1) being eight years old again or 2) chopping off your toes.

_____

19,999,999

Hmmm. That leaves one eligible man out of 125 million. But take heart! Our crack research department has identified him. He is one Lester D. Calvados, a lumberjack living in the forests of the Pacific Northwest. Via telephone Lester told us—in his deep, manly voice—that he'd be delighted to have you, as a single woman, come see him but that you'll have to pay your own way because he's saving his money to go to Sweden for an operation.

So, clearly this example tells us two things:

1. Finding the right mate isn't so easy after all.
2. Lester is going to look simply lovely in plaid flannel evening gowns.

OPPOSITES DETRACT

It seems that these days the more that men and women try, the more they know about human psychology, and the more books and seminars about love they have completed, the less they can stay together. Why? Well, the most obvious handicaps are the differences between the genders. Here again we see the trade-off that comes with everything from Mother Nature (the bitter old crone). For example, a day at the beach means sun, sand, and surf. But it also means fat men in Speedos. Rain makes the flowers grow. But it also cancels your golf game.

Chocolate tastes great. But it goes straight to the thighs of fat men in Speedos.

And so it is with men and women. We are different. That attracts us to each other, but that also drives us crazy.

Here are a few differences that run fairly true along gender lines:

Men are more violent and aggressive than women are. This difference has been a big factor in human history. For example, the War of the Roses was thirty years of bloodshed. If women had been running the world in 1455, the War of the Roses would have been just a slap fight between two florists.

Women have taste; men have tattoos. Women grasp the subtleties of color; men grasp the subtleties of celebrity bass fishing.

Men don't feel comfortable in places that stress color selection. Such as clothing, department, and linen stores. They feel awkward and out of their element, like a woman reporter feels in a men's team locker room. She just wants to get her story and get out of there before she steps on a protective cup.

Women select furnishings and clothes based on colors that complement each other; men select furnishings and clothes based on which colors won't show pizza stains.

For this reason, women typically are better dressers than men are. Men will wear most anything. Unnatural colors, unnatural patterns, unnatural fabrics. This is why the science of cryogenics was developed—so that after men die they could be frozen and then thawed out and brought back to life when a cure is found for their wardrobes.

A woman is more apt than a man to remember minute details about personal special occasions—what both of them were wearing on their first date, what movie they saw, what they ate, little things that they said. The man may not remember such details, even though he can remember sports statistics dating back to the Paleozoic era, when most professional sports were dominated by reptiles.

ALTARS AND ANTLERS

A man and a woman are likely to approach their wedding differently. The woman will put more planning into the ceremony than the Allies put into the D-Day invasion of Europe. But then the Allies didn't also have to worry about finding just the right organist.

On the big day, if her pastel gown, makeup, hair, and nails and those of her bridesmaids are anything less than perfect, God and *Glamour* forbid, she will have no choice but to excuse herself politely from the altar, rush out of the church, and throw herself under a pastel Mack truck.

The man, on the other hand, may come to the church straight from a hunting trip, still carrying a rifle and wearing a camouflage outfit gaily festooned with deer parts. The mortified woman who is about to take such a man for better or for worse, through sickness and health, 'til venison do them part, must remember three things: 1. this man is, despite his present appearance, still the man she fell in love with; 2. she *will* get over this humiliating experience, assuming that she lives to be three hundred; and 3. she would be wise not to wear antlers at the reception.

A man and a woman are also likely to approach *things* differently. Men value a thing for itself and want to know how it works. Women value a thing for its usefulness to them and aren't as concerned about how it works.

For example, if a man and a woman look at a car, the man will wonder if the engine is six or eight cylinders, and if six, if it is in-line or V, and what kind of cams and lifters and carburetor and so on it has, until he begins to breathe heavily and drool STP.

The woman will look at that same car and ask only if it will get her where she wants to go, which is usually as far away as possible from that drooling man. Not that women, too, can't become attached to their cars. And certainly, being sentimental and detail-oriented, a woman may associate a particular make and model of car with times and people in her past. If back in high school her boyfriend broke up with her in his red '70 Chevy Malibu Super Sport, many years later if she sees such a car, it will trigger an emotional response, and she will relive the hurt and loss. She will whimper, curl up into the fetal position, and begin to softly hum a medley of old Carpenters' songs.

Similarly, women look at a computer and ask: "What can I do with it?" Men look at a computer and ask the speed of its processor chip. For men, processor speed is the new horsepower, the '90s measure of masculinity. If a man's computer has a processor speed of 75, but his buddy's computer has 133, the first man will suffer from what Freud called processor envy. He feels vaguely inferior, inadequate. And if a third man has a computer with a speed of 166, the first two men avert their eyes respectfully when he walks by and offer to polish his briefcase.

Men and women have different approaches to shopping. For example, while grocery shopping a woman has a list, but she also relies on inspiration. She may commune with the fresh vegetables. She may develop a deeply personal relationship with the cheeses. Ultimately, she buys the cheddar, but she makes the mozzarella promise to write.

Men don't shop at a supermarket so much as they make an assault on it. They are in and out in six minutes. They may go in with a list, but no matter what is on the list, they always buy the same two items: beer and potato chips.

EAU DE QUICKY MART

Men and women have different approaches to giving a gift to a mate. A woman puts a lot of thought into buying a gift. She considers her mate's age, weight, hair and eye color, blood type, personality, interests, astrological sign, the phase of the moon, relative humidity, and the speed of his processor chip. Then she selects *the* perfect gift to give him.

A man gives perfume.

Which he buys at a convenience store.

Oh, a man may *want* to give a woman something more personal and intimate, like a frilly bra. But men are not very good at knowing women's sizes. And yet this is the same gender that, at a glance, can tell the length of a baseball bat, the gauge of a shotgun, and the diameter of a piston.

So he goes to a lingerie store, where he feels both awkward and aroused, and approaches a saleswoman:

Saleswoman (pleasantly): "What size does the lady wear?"

Man (at a loss): "Uh. I dunno. But she's ..." (begins to make vaguely rounded shapes in the air with his hands).

Saleswoman (puzzled): "The lady is a cantaloupe?"

Man (flustered, trying not to look anywhere below the saleswoman's eyes for helpful comparison): "No. Oh, just give me a quart of perfume."

When he presents his gift to his mate, she feigns delight ("Gee...perfume") while taking it from him like it is a live snake. Later she throws the bottle into a closet filled with other bottles of perfume that he has given her. Tragically, one day she opens the closet door, and all those bottles come crashing down on her in an avalanche of glass. The last thing that she sees in this life is a perfume label that reads: "May also be used as a herbicide."

He Said, She Said

Mrs. Claus: "Yeah, but when was the last time he gave *me* anything?"

Women express their feelings more readily than men do. Men will freely talk about sports, politics, current events, work, but not feelings. As you know if you've ever had a cricket somewhere in your home and tried to find it, crickets stop chirping just when you get close to them. It's a defense mechanism. Men are like that—they stop chirping when you get close to them.

Women also often complain about this: Men are ready for sex sooner—but ready for a commitment later—than women are. Timing is everything in a relationship. Often a man and a woman are out of synch. Typically, a man is ready for sex approximately two minutes after meeting a woman (four minutes if he is getting a tattoo at the time). But later, when she is ready to marry him, he may not be ready. Typically, a man realizes that he is ready to marry a woman the minute that he hears that she has given up on him and married another man.

Men more than women turn to physical intimacy to solve relationship difficulties. Whereas a woman needs time and communication to regain psychological and physical closeness with a man after an argument, a man is more apt to say, "I don't care what you say, you're still wrong. Wrong. Wrong. Wrong. You incredible imbecile. Now let's get naked."

(An Ohio man holds the record for such a quick shift of mental gears. One moment he was having an argument with his wife that resembled a scene from an "Itchy & Scratchy" cartoon. Twenty-seven seconds later he was asking her to smear his body with lard.)

Because of such differences, at some point it occurs to each of us that every man and woman should come with a label. You know—like those for laundry care on clothes or those surgeon general's health warnings on cigarettes or those window stickers on new cars:

> **Directions for care:** This woman is made of highly unstable material. Handle gently. Do not press. When in hot water, likely to run.
>
> **Warning:** The four ex-wives of this man have determined that he may be hazardous to your mental health, and watch that first kiss in the morning.

Equipment on this model: *Standard:* 2 legs, 2 arms, 1 navel (innie). *Optional:* 2 blue eyes, IQ of 123, 24-inch waist, 4-speed libido with overdrive. *Estimated mileage between mood swings:* 16.8 city, 23.4 highway

Perhaps the greatest handicap to lasting love is time. Time changes people. Sometimes this change is called "growing as a person," sometimes it is called "drifting apart," sometimes it is called "turning into an insufferable old bitch." As the months or years pass, two people change until they are no longer the people they fell in love with. They no longer share the interests or attitudes that attracted them to each other.

If we could just make time stand still, we could make love last. Also, milk would never be past its expiration date.

Time has another effect: Just as running water in a brook eventually wears smooth the sharp edges of a pebble, so does time wear smooth the sharp edges of passion. Familiarity breeds contempt, Aesop said. And he should know. In the beginning of their marriage, Mrs. Aesop would summon him to bed each night by coming into the den and dancing provocatively as he sat reading. It drove him wild in the beginning. But then one day the night came when she came into the den while Aesop was reading and danced provocatively, and he said, "Honey, please. You're in my light."

Also, as time passes and the flame of early love cools, we see each other more clearly, more objectively. We notice little flaws, little irritants in the other that we never noticed before. "Gee," a woman says to herself, "I had never realized how mean-spirited Delbert is. And it's funny that I had never noticed that he has a mole on his ear. And that he has a tail and antennae."

Things That You Can Be Sure of after
Breaking Up with Someone

☞ She will discover that all along she was a latent nympho-maniac.

☞ He will finally figure out what "foreplay" means.

☞ His skin will clear up.

☞ She will lose twenty pounds.

☞ He will finally give up on the Nehru jacket.

☞ She will find her one true hair color and stick with it.

☞ He will win the lottery.

☞ She will discover that she likes football.

☞ You will see her out with someone younger, taller, and handsomer.

☞ You will see him out with someone younger, thinner, prettier, and dumber.

BEAVIN' IS BELIEVIN'

Sometimes we sabotage our relationships by having unreasonable expectations. The expectations that baby boomers have about marriage were influenced by the couples in family-based TV comedies of the '50s and '60s: *Leave It to Beaver, Ozzie and Harriet, Father Knows Best, The Donna Reed Show*. These couples consisted of a sweater-wearing, pipe-smoking, mild-mannered husband who was always at home and a mild-mannered mother who wore an apron and pearls and baked cookies. These couples never drank, never cheated, never had moods, never sweated. They never had *any* bodily functions. They simply exploded during the rerun season.

No wonder baby boomers are disappointed in their spouses. "Harriet wouldn't treat Ozzie that way," they whine.

And "I'll bet that Mr. Knows Best would shower for Mrs. Knows Best."

We all have an image of the ideal mate, based on our other-sex parent, movie stars, heroes of fairy tales, and popular culture. But these images are impossible amalgams. A man may compare all of his dates with a perfect woman, who has the looks of Julia Roberts, the wisdom of Sandra Day O'Connor, and the vacuous charm of Vanna White. A woman may hold all men up to her fantasy man, who has the honor of her father, the humor of Seinfeld, the gentleness of Gandhi, and the body of Schwarzenegger. No wonder she gives up on every man who can't clean and jerk 200 pounds while meditating in the lotus position.

Things That Men Would Rush into a Burning House to Rescue

- ☞ Power tools
- ☞ Dog
- ☞ Collection of baseball cards and Billy Beer
- ☞ Back issues of *Field & Stream*, *Car & Driver*, and *Chicks & Chains*
- ☞ Softball league trophy ("Most Improved Bunter")
- ☞ Videocassette of sports bloopers (on Beta)
- ☞ Victoria's Secret catalogue

Things That Women Would Rush into a Burning House to Rescue

- ☞ Hair dryer
- ☞ Cat
- ☞ Back issues of *Cosmo*

☞ Her African violets, especially Timmy, the sickly one

☞ Every love letter she has ever received, dating back to third grade

☞ Preserved prom mums, theater ticket stubs, slice of wedding cake

☞ The one suit she owns that actually fits the way it should

☞ Victoria's Secret catalogue

Sometimes we sabotage our chances of love by becoming too cautious after a bad experience with the opposite sex. We generalize. Of course, generalizing can be very handy in life. For example, after you learn how to drive one specific car, you can generalize from that how to drive most any car. After you learn how to walk up one specific flight of stairs, you can generalize from that how much you prefer to take the elevator. But generalization can be self-defeating in our personal relationships. If one or two men are mean to you, don't generalize that all men are mean. If, however, ninety or one hundred men are mean to you, you might be entitled to generalize that all men are mean. You might also consider taking that "KICK ME" sign off your back.

A thousand years ago, life was simpler for men and women. There was less to disagree about. You and your mate lived in a crude stone hut with a dirt floor, and you both performed manual labor for an omnipotent feudal lord who paid you in gruel, and you died of old age at forty.

How much better life is today. Today when you work overtime, you get paid gruel and a half.

But life also is much more complicated today. There are more stresses, more temptations, more choices, more changes. One of the biggest changes in our culture is the women's revolution. Women are making long-overdue advances, getting their own circles of friends, their own beepers and cell phones, their own bank accounts, careers, and perforated ulcers.

Roles are changing and even reversing. Millions of wives have fulfilling careers outside the home. A husband even may stay home, taking care of the children—usually in the form of feeding the baby onion dip strained through a sock—and performing such duties as washing and cleaning and dusting. The wife comes home at the end of the day and makes a martini while the husband tells her about his day. "And did you dust the mantelpiece?" she asks. The husband looks at her and asks, "We have a mantelpiece?"

WAKE UP AND SMELL THE CHANEL

But as women's lives improve, both genders go through a period of adjustment. As rules and roles change, confusion and ambivalence result. A man may not be sure how a woman wants to be treated. A *woman* may not be sure how she wants to be treated. Does a man open a door for her? Does he bring her flowers, or is that sexist? Should he instead bring her a token of his esteem that is more gender-neutral? Dental floss, perhaps.

Some men have difficulty letting go of the past and relating to women as equals who are not to be placed on a pedestal, repressed, or possessed. Likewise, women are having to learn to see themselves as equals who don't have to be owned or intimidated by men. When a woman finds herself feeling intimidated by a man—a date, a coworker, a potential employer—she should imagine him wearing nothing but a pair of black socks. She'll never see him the same way again. Black socks are part of the standard business attire of a man. When a man pulls on a pair of black socks, he just naturally develops an urge to write a memo or declare a stock dividend or trade noogies with Lee Iacocca. Such attire lets him feel and appear powerful and intimidating, just like the Wizard of Oz, who was really just a short little weenie standing on a crate and using a megaphone.

But when you imagine that same man without the rest of his business attire, wearing *only* those black socks, he looks pale and puny and sorta plucked. He no longer has his crate and megaphone, and you just automatically want to:

1. Laugh at him.

2. Give the little boy in him a motherly hug.

3. Give the little boy in him a motherly hug and stick that "KICK ME" sign on his back.

What can be done to ease relations between the genders? Not much. But leading relationship experts, many of whom we just made up, recommend that you:

Forget the Golden Rule. Do unto your mate as he or she wants to be done unto, not as you would want to be done unto.

For example, if you like to be pampered with attention, but your mate likes to be allowed to pull her own weight, solve her own problems, and do for herself, don't insist on pushing her shopping cart, carrying her luggage, and rotating her tires. She'll appreciate the restraint, and you can save that hernia for softball season.

Little Things That Lovers Can Do unto Each Other

- ☞ Give him a fishing knife with your name engraved on it. Every time he guts a crappie, he'll think of you.
- ☞ Just once, when the two of you eat out, don't insist on arm-wrestling the waiter for the check.
- ☞ Write her a love letter that does not have the word *knockers* in it.
- ☞ Write him a love letter that does not have the word *love* in it.

Accept the differences. Don't expect a man to think and feel like a woman; don't expect a woman to think and feel like a man. On the other hand, recognize that no person is totally one gender. Men have a feminine side, women have a masculine side. For example, you just *know* that sometimes around the Gifford household, Kathie Lee wants to put on Frank's old shoulder pads and crouch down into the "set" position. And in the Heloise household, sometimes Mr. Heloise surely wants to dispense advice on how to get candle wax out of the carpet. ("First, guys, move a piece of furniture over the candle wax. A sofa will do. Sit on the sofa. Have a beer. Your work is done. Spilled some beer on the sofa? Cover the stain with some candle wax.")

On the other hand, don't automatically attribute a person's behavior to his or her gender. Some people would be jerks as a man *or* a woman. They would be jerks if they were a vegetable. In a salad, they'd be rude to the other vegetables. They would insult the lettuce. They would make the poor cucumbers cry.

Signs That Your Mate Is Turning to Other Sources for Companionship

☞ Comes home and asks the cat how its day was.
☞ Begins giving you the dog's scraps.
☞ Has more pet names for the pet than for you.
☞ Establishes a trust fund for his bass boat.
☞ Models lingerie for the vacuum cleaner.
☞ Mentally undresses the houseplants.
☞ When listing next of kin, names bartender.
☞ Visits his prostate surgeon between scheduled exams.

Try to compromise. John Stuart Mill's philosophy of Utilitarianism held "those actions right which promote the greatest happiness of the greatest number" in a community. Think of a couple as a community of two. If you can do something that will benefit your two-person community by fifty units but that will cost you only twenty-five units of time or effort or swallowed pride, go for it.

DUGOUTS AND DIVAS

For example, get involved in your partner's interests. Let's say that you are a woman who doesn't care for baseball, but your mate does. Go to a game with him. Ask him to help you understand and appreciate the action:

She: "What's happening now?"

He: "Well, nothing. The pitcher is manicuring the mound. But wait just a second."

She: "What's happening now?"

He: "Well, nothing. The batter is going through his loosening-up ritual. But wait just a second."

She: "What's happening now?"

He: "Well, nothing. The catcher and pitcher are conferring on the mound. But wait just a second."

Yes, with your husband's guidance, you will learn that in baseball, what takes place between the action is very important, that anticipation and nuance are everything.

"What's the batter doing now?"

"He's scratching his groin."

"Is that anticipation or nuance?"

With your husband's guidance, you will learn to understand the elaborate signals of the third base coach as he tugs on his ears, slaps his thighs, wipes his arms, and pats his chest.

"What does all that mean?"

"Well, the coach either is telling the batter to take the next pitch or asking the batter out for dinner and slow dancing after the game."

"Oh, I do hope it's the latter. They seem made for each other."

Likewise, if you are a man who hates opera, but your mate loves it, skip a ball game one night and go to an opera with her, keep an open mind, and share her pleasure:

"Okay. We're here. Now tell me what I am going to see."

"First, read your program. See—this opera is called *Ein Schnitzel fur Griselda*. Setting: the German village of Fahrvergnugen. Time: the Middle Ages, about 2 P.M. Now, as the curtain rises, the orchestra plays the overture, setting the tone of the drama. Listen: The woodwinds are dark and foreboding; the brasses are moody and ominous; the strings are bright and cheery." (Several bars into the overture the strings realize that they have the wrong sheet music.)

"Now Act I is beginning. That woman is Griselda, the beautiful-yet-humble village girl who has but one tragic flaw— she is named Griselda. She is at the village well, singing a sad soliloquy about how when she was a baby her domineering father, Wolfram, arranged her marriage to old Ludwig, who is ninety-three but who by age seven already was called 'old Ludwig.' With thirty-seven deutsche marks and the world's largest privately held collection of tongue depressors, old Ludwig is the village's wealthiest man. But Griselda loves only Sigfried, the young butcher's apprentice. She is singing of how she longs to dance barefoot with Sigfried in a large platter of sliced veal—seasoned, garnished, and lightly breaded.

"And who's that guy?"

"That's Sigfried. He has entered to sing a response to Griselda's desire to dance in veal. He is asking her if she has been taking her medication regularly."

"Now what are they saying?"

"They are singing a tender duet about their ill-fated love while behind them someone in the chorus is having a coughing fit."

"Now what?"

"Now it's Act II: The wedding day has drawn nigh. In her room, in a touching aria, Griselda is singing of how she does not love old Ludwig and dreads a lifetime of helping him cut his food."

"Who is that man?"

"That's Wolfram, Griselda's father, an unattractive man with an overbite and strudel on his chin. He has entered to sing boldly of his determination that the wedding proceed as arranged. Now we in the audience are being given month-old produce to hurl at him. If we had seats in the first three rows, we'd be given automatic weapons."

"Now what? Where are we going?"

"We're getting up. This is the intermission."

"Oh. The seventh-inning stretch."

"Okay, now we're back as Act III begins: The wedding is about to begin. That's Brunhilda, goddess of love. She is intervening. She conjures up a thunderstorm and, with the help of Lederhosen, the god of leather shorts often worn with suspenders, directs a lightning bolt to weld Wolfram's zipper shut. Wolfram will spend the rest of Act III hopping up and down and wishing he hadn't just drunk that barrel of bock. But he also sees the error of his ways and frees Griselda of the marriage contract."

"Now what are they doing?"

"The entire village has gathered in the square, and Griselda and Sigfried are being wed. As the curtain rings down, all dance and sing joyously. Old Ludwig falls and breaks his hip.

"And that's it. You've seen your first opera. What do you think?"

"I think Cal Ripken Jr. woulda made a better Sigfried."

FEUD FOR THOUGHT

Don't fight. In a relationship no one "wins" a fight. What the individual gains, the relationship loses. Granted, resisting an argument can be difficult when people are determined to argue. They will hang an argument on any pretext:

"Honey, I'm home. How was your day?"

"Just what do you mean by *that* crack?"

At such times there's no use in your being logical. Here's an exchange that occurred between Chaucer and his wife in 1386:

"You left the cap off the toothpaste again, didn't you?"

"But toothpaste hasn't even been invented yet!"

"Well, just don't let it happen again."

The most innocent, peaceful exchange can become heated and lead to words that never should have been said. It may begin as a discussion, but before either person realizes what is happening, it has become a voice-raising, finger-pointing, door-slamming, tear-wiping civil war. The neighbors cringe. Dogs howl. CBS correspondent Bob Simon provides daily updates on the evening news.

Keep the big picture. Many times a word or a deed that seems so hurtful and all-consuming and life-threatening right now will barely be remembered in a year:

"Honey, what was it that you and I got into that big fight about last year, and the argument got so out of control that National Guardsmen were parachuted in to contain its spread by setting back-arguments?"

"Gee, I can't remember, Dear. But weren't those the nicest young men?"

Subjects That Men and Women Most Commonly Disagree On

☞ Money
☞ Parenting
☞ Choice of vacation destinations
☞ Choice of TV viewing
☞ How drunk he was the night he proposed
☞ The intelligence, intentions, and personal hygiene of each other's friends
☞ His theory about the cultural contribution made to Western civilization by lap dancing
☞ Her theory that foreplay should last longer than a TV commercial but that an engagement should not last longer than Susan Lucci has been waiting for an Emmy

Don't try to change your mate. This is a common complaint among men—that women try to change them. But you seldom can change how a person thinks and feels. At best you change only how a person acts; at worst you create resentment. Change must come from within. So don't try to change that man, no matter how much just a minor tweak in him here and there would improve his appearance, your sex life, the air quality, and the GNP.

Be yourself. You can't trick someone into being attracted to you by pretending to be something that you are not. It catches up with you. Padding your personality works about as well as padding your bra with Kleenex or your pants with a roll of quarters: Eventually you go out with someone who asks you for a tissue or change for a dollar.

Don't be possessive. Love is like an ice cube: If you hold it loosely in the hollow of your hand, it will warm and melt to fit and stay put. But if you squeeze love possessively, it will squirt through your fingers, fall to the floor, skid under the bed, and get covered with lint. And no one wants linty love.

Mother Goose Update

Peter, Peter Pumpkin-Eater
Had a wife and couldn't keep her.
Put her in a pumpkin shell
And there he kept her very well.

THE PUMPKIN PATCH — Peter P. Pumpkin-Eater, 47, was found dead at his home today, a jack-o'-lantern smashed over his head.

Police investigating the slaying told reporters that pumpkin seeds next to the body spelled out "Free at last." Pumpkin-Eater's wife, Shirley, confessed and was taken into custody, claiming years of neglect, repression, and mental anguish from a man whom she described as being "out of his gourd."

"Pete would never let me go out. He was so insecure and possessive. He kept me in that darned pumpkin shell under lock and key twenty-four hours a day. Sure, he let me decorate it, and it was quite stylish with accent lamps and some throw rugs and a divine little Louis IV armoire that I bought from a catalogue. But there's just so much you can do with a pumpkin.

"And if that weren't enough, all he ever brought me to eat was pumpkins—pumpkin pies, pumpkin cookies, pumpkin sandwiches, pumpkin hash. Finally I couldn't take it anymore. I tunneled out, using a spoon he gave me to eat pumpkin chili, and attacked him in his sleep. He got what he deserved. He ruined my life. I have no friends. I have no self-esteem. I have no social skills. And I can't see the color orange without freaking out."

Mrs. Pumpkin-Eater was released on bond but was rejailed a few hours later at a service station after going berserk beneath the "Gulf" sign.

Newton's law of physics states that two bodies cannot occupy the same space at the same time. But that is just what we sometimes try to do in a relationship. "You" and "I" try to merge into a new entity: "we." We become indivisible, submerging our twoness in our oneness. Pain results when, over time, we two don't remain as one as we had begun. Maybe we shouldn't expect so much from love with another person. Another person can do a great many things for us: tune up our car, iron our clothes, kiss us until we see our ancestors, God, and Elvis in a brilliant light at the end of a tunnel. But another person can't make us happy, can't make us like ourselves or be content with who we are. Being happy is the ultimate do-it-yourself project. A happy you is something that you have to build yourself.

Of course, it's pretty neat to have someone special there to hand you the hammer.

The Doctor Is In

It's time again to ask Dr. Romance:

Q. When did the custom of divorce begin?

A. In A.D. 450 the first divorce on record was granted to Attila the Hun and his wife, Eunice the Hun. The judge granted Attila custody of Germany, but Eunice was allowed to pillage Bavaria on weekends and holidays.

Q. My boyfriend just broke up with me, and so I went out and spent twelve hundred dollars on clothes. Why did I do that?

A. After two people break up, at least one of them typically goes through the five stages of grieving: denial, anger, bargaining, depression, and shopping. Yes, heartache often drives us to shop. When we hurt, we want the mind-numbing diversion of a new toy, some material excess to fill the spiritual void. Malls thrive on busted romances. At any given time, 24 percent of people at the mall are there to buy anesthesia for a broken heart. They seek something expensive and totally unnecessary: a sports car, a motorcycle, furniture, stereo and video equipment, one of the smaller states. Clothes are a favorite purchase of the brokenhearted. A person can go through his or her clothes closet and find a chronology of lost love: "This jacket I bought in 1989 after Cathy broke up with me. This suit I bought in 1991 after Jennifer dumped me. And these elevator shoes I bought in 1994 after Bonnie left me for a Boston Celtic."

Q.   After all is said and done, is love the answer?

A.   Yes. Assuming that the question is: "What makes a person have sweaty palms, heart palpitations, dizzy spells, loss of appetite, insomnia, and shortness of breath?" This is why Dr. Romance finds it helpful to date registered nurses.

Epilogue

United We Stand, Divided We Pay Divorce Lawyers

CAN WOMEN AND MEN ever really understand and relate to each other, you ask. Is there any hope for compatibility when the two genders look at something as neutral as mud, and one gender sees a beauty pack for the face, and the other gender sees a medium for college girls to wrestle in?

Certainly there may be times when we despair of finding and keeping love with the other gender. There may be times when we swear off the other gender entirely after a bad date or a bad marriage. But our resolve doesn't last long. Soon, when we least expect it, we're at a bingo parlor when we see an enchanting face across the cards. Or we're in a classroom when an intriguing voice says to us: "Excuse me. Is this where freshman biology meets?"

Soon we're head over heels again, laughing, loving, dissecting earthworms.

Somewhere amid all this, Mother Nature is laughing out loud. She has really outdone herself in making men and women hopelessly attracted to each other. Why did she do her job so well? Perhaps because she's been there. Because she, too, is single. After all, you never hear anything about Father Nature. Where is he? What happened to him, huh? Don't ask Mother Nature. Every time the subject comes up, she begins to weep softly. Soon there are monsoons in India.

Ultimately, all that men and women have is each other. That is our blessing. That is our curse. It's a good thing that we're stuck *on* each other, because we're also stuck *with* each other.

Maybe recognition of this bittersweet fact will enable women and men of Earth—descendants of those brave voyagers from Pluto and Uranus—to go hand in hand as we stroll into the twenty-first century. Don't forget to take along your Binaca, stand up straight, smile, be yourself, walk on the sunny side of the street, consult your physician if symptoms persist, and remember: If love is the answer, you must have misunderstood the question.

Still, you just gotta keep asking.